RAP LYRICS

FROM THE SUGARHILL GANG TO EMINEM

WISE PUBLICATIONS
in association with
 OMNIBUS PRESS
www.omnibuspress.com

Exclusive Distributors:
Music Sales Limited
8/9 Frith Street, London W1D 3JB, England.
Music Sales Pty Limited
120 Rothschild Avenue, Rosebery, NSW 2018, Australia.

Order No. AM971993
ISBN 0-7119-9071-9
This book © Copyright 2002 by Wise Publications.

Compiled and transcribed by Alex Ogg.
Artist biographies by Alex Ogg.
Project editor: James Sleigh.

Cover & book design by Phil Gambrill @ Fresh Lemon.

Photo Credits:
Front & back cover: LFI; Piers Allardyce/SIN: 33; David Corio/SIN: 15;
Melanie Cox/SIN: 85; Joe Dilworth/SIN: 53; Martyn Goodacre/SIN: 70;
LFI:1, 5, 12, 17, 18, 20, 21, 22, 25, 26, 27, 28, 29, 34, 36, 37, 39, 44, 45, 47, 50, 52, 57,
58, 59, 60, 64, 67, 68, 73, 76, 78, 80, 82, 88, 91, 92, 94, 96; Chi Modu/Redferns: 63;
Erik Pendzich/Rex: 8; Alessio Pizzicannella/SIN: 74; Leo Regan/SIN: 48;
Ebet Roberts /Redferns: 16, 30; Nicky J. Sims/Redferns: 11; Ian T. Tilton/SIN: 40, 54.

Printed in the United Kingdom by Caligraving Limited, Thetford, Norfolk.

Your Guarantee of Quality:
As publishers, we strive to produce every book to the highest commercial standards.
Particular care has been given to specifying acid-free, neutral-sized
paper made from pulps which have not been elemental chlorine bleached.
This pulp is from farmed sustainable forests and was produced
with special regard for the environment.
Throughout, the printing and binding have been planned to ensure a sturdy,
attractive publication which should give years of enjoyment.
If your copy fails to meet our high standards, please inform us and
we will gladly replace it.

Music Sales' complete catalogue describes thousands of titles and
is available in full colour sections by subject, direct from Music Sales Limited.
Please state your areas of interest and send a cheque/postal order for £1.50 for postage to:
Music Sales Limited, Newmarket Road, Bury St. Edmunds, Suffolk IP33 3YB.

www.musicsales.com

ACKNOWLEDGEMENTS

The author would like to thank his partner Dawn Wrench, David Upshal
and commissioning and project editor James Sleigh.
He would also like to praise the work of the
Original Hip Hop Lyrics Archive (www.ohhla.com) for providing
a comprehensive survey of rap lyrics past and present,
against which the final transcriptions for the book were checked.

If you love lyrics, or, like this author, derived much of your education from vinyl rather than folio, then hip hop, acknowledged by *Time* magazine as the 'single most important cultural phenomenon of the past quarter-century', presents a uniquely stimulating and fertile forum. There are more words than a conventional rock lyric, for a start. The Sugarhill Gang's 'Rapper's Delight' saw 'those brothers who rock so viciously' do just that for nearly 3,000 words and 17 minutes. But while I would advise no-one to spend a significant portion of their life analysing the nuances of that particular effort, it did establish hip hop as the perfect platform for the contemporary wordsmith. Despite all evidence to the contrary,

Hip hop's brief history, in keeping with the cut and paste aesthetic of the music, rarely offers a smooth continuum. The ultimate post-modern genre, it deconstructs the familiar, hunting down useful snatches of sound from unlikely sources in order to reassemble what it finds in new and unpredictable ways, a benevolent parasite leaping from one host culture to the next. So while many of the lyrics in this book reference each other, the chronology is obscured by shifts back and forward through time, in and out of different musical genres and styles. As ever, licensing constraints meant we couldn't always get exactly what we wanted, so Notorious B.I.G., Jay-Z, Nas and DMX may have to wait for a second volume.

After 'Rapper's Delight', Kurtis Blow's 'The Breaks' confirmed that there was mileage in what many assumed was a novelty craze, while Grandmaster Flash's 'The Message' argued that the subject matter need not be one-dimensional. But it was with the

INTRODUCTION

rap is still criticised as a reductive, degenerative musical form, readily dismissed by reference to some admittedly regrettable lyrics (a selection of which are included in this book). But dismissing an art form based on its more infantile manifestations is folly on a par with branding country music 'redneck'.

It's worth pointing out immediately that this book is meant to complement the records it discusses, rather than replace them. No bare-page transcription will ever convey the ping-pong theatricals of Run-D.M.C.'s call and response interplay, the way the Bomb Squad emboss Chuck D's savage rhetoric on Public Enemy's records or the rhyme patterns, delivery or cadences that make individual MCs unique.

arrival of Run-D.M.C. that hip hop was reborn as rap, the dynamic eschewing acoustic niceties in favour of rugged, fist-hard battle rhymes. They even dispensed with the bass line. A music that had formerly embraced the fantastic, the futuristic and the escapist, now professed to 'keeping it real'.

Along with Run-D.M.C., the mid-80s were dominated by Def Jam's touchstone acts, LL Cool J, the Beastie Boys and Public Enemy. LL was rap's first b-boy superstar, who told it like it was with enough surplus natural charisma to win over pop audiences after conquering the hip hop market. The Beasties were white interlopers whose open hostility to mainstream values saw them embraced by resentful suburban teenagers the world over. Public Enemy, rap's most important soothsayers, seethed and scowled and used words as projectiles to be launched against the status quo. In Chuck D they had a lyricist whose ability to articulate resentment and indignation surpassed any who had preceded him. The black Johnny Rotten? And then some.

Others such as Eric B and Rakim, Gang Starr and
Boogie Down Productions played pivotal roles in
expanding hip hop's musical and linguistic frontiers.
But away from hip hop's traditional birthing grounds
in New York, something ugly was brewing on the west
coast of America. N.W.A.'s indiscriminate hate-speak
was succinctly expressed in their full billing Niggers
With Attitude. Their tales of arbitrary gangland
violence saw them become pin-ups in every teenage

This book concludes with some of rap's latest
crop - southern-ballers OutKast, the multi-talented
Missy Elliott, pop-gangsta Puff Daddy and Eminem.
The first star MC of the 21st century, Eminem has tied
many of hip hop's disparate threads together.
A virtuoso lyricist, his skills are honed on a rigid
belief in the importance of 'freestyling' – a throwback
to the combative party duels that kick-started the
original hip hop phenomenon.

white suburban bedroom whilst incensing everyone
from the liberal intelligentsia to the FBI. Gangsta rap
had one hand in the cash register and the other
around the throat of mainstream American culture.
But for all the escalating misanthropy of the
phenomenon, there were also great records. The best
ones invariably had former N.W.A. member Dr Dre's
prints on them somewhere, while the pre-eminent
rappers included Snoop Doggy Dogg and Tupac
Shakur. The latter began to roll with Death Row just
as the most infamous label in the music business
started to live up to its name.

Any such survey of an art form can only be
representative, at best. But there is some attempt to
trace the chronological development of the rap lyric,
whilst making the occasional detour to acknowledge
particularly noteworthy developments or efforts of
special historical significance.

[Wonder Mike]
I said-a hip hop, the hippie the hippie
To the hip hip hop, a-you don't stop
The rock it to the bang bang boogie say up
jumped the boogie
To the rhythm of the boogie, the beat
Now what you hear is not a test –
I'm rappin' to the beat
And me, the groove, and my friends
are gonna try to move your feet
See I am Wonder Mike and I'd like to say hello
To the black, to the white, the red, and
the brown, the purple and yellow
But first I gotta bang bang the boogie to the boogie
Say up jump the boogie to the bang bang boogie
Let's rock, you don't stop
Rock the rhythm that will make your body rock
Well so far you've heard my voice but
I brought two friends along
And next on the mic is my man Hank

Everybody go hotel motel whatcha gonna
do today (say what?)
Ya say I'm gonna get a fly girl,
gonna get some spankin'
Drive off in a def OJ
Everybody go, hotel motel Holiday Inn
Say if your girl starts actin' up,
then you take her friend
Master Gee, am I mellow?
It's on you, so what you gonna do?

[Master Gee]
Well it's on-n on-n on on-n on
The beat don't stop until the break of dawn
I said m-a-s, t-e-r, a g with a double e
I said I go by the unforgettable name
Of the man they call the Master Gee
Well, my name is known all over the world

SUGARHILL GANG
RAPPER'S DELIGHT
RELEASED: 1979. INCLUDED ON RAPPER'S DELIGHT: THE BEST OF THE SUGARHILL GANG (1996)

Come on, Hank, sing that song.

[Big Bank Hank]
Check it out, I'm the c-a-s-an-the-o-v-a
And the rest is f-l-y
Ya see I go by the code of the doctor of the mix
And these reasons I'll tell ya why
Ya see I'm six foot one and I'm tons of fun
And I dress to a 't'
Ya see I got more clothes than Muhammad Ali
and I dress so viciously
I got bodyguards, I got two big cars
That definitely ain't the wack
I got a Lincoln Continental and a sunroof Cadillac
So after school, I take a dip in the pool
Which is really on the wall
I got a colour TV so I can see
The Knicks play basketball
Hear me talkin' bout chequebooks, credit cards
More money than a sucker could ever spend
But I wouldn't give a sucker or a bum
from the rucker
Not a dime till I made it again

By all the foxy ladies and the pretty girls
I'm goin' down in history
As the baddest rapper there ever could be
Now I'm feelin' the highs and ya feelin' the lows
The beat starts getting' into your toes
Ya start poppin' ya fingers and stompin' your feet
And movin' your body while you're sittin'
in your seat
And then damn, ya start doin' the freak
I said damn, right outta your seat
Then ya throw your hands high in the air
Ya rockin' to the rhythm, shake your derriere
Ya rockin' to the beat without a care
With the sureshot MCs for the affair
Now, I'm not as tall as the rest of the gang
But I rap to the beat just the same
I got a little face and a pair of brown eyes
All I'm here to do ladies is hypnotise
Singin' on-n-n on-n on-n on
The beat don't stop until the break of dawn
Singin' on-n-n on-n on on-n on
Like a hot buttered a-pop-da-pop da-pop
dibbie dibbie
Pop da pop pop ya don't dare stop
Come alive y'all, gimme what ya got

I guess by now you can take a hunch
And find that I am the baby of the bunch
But that's OK, I still keep in stride
Cause all I'm here to do is just boogie your behind
Singin on-n-n on-n on-n on
The beat don't stop until the break of dawn
Singin' on-n-n on-n on on-n on
Rock rock y'all, throw it on the floor
I'm gonna freak ya here, I'm gonna freak ya there
I'm gonna move you outta this atmosphere
Cos I'm one of a kind and I'll shock your mind
I'll put t-t-tickets in your behind
I said 1-2-3-4, come on girls get on the floor
A-come alive, y'all, a-gimme what ya got
Cos I'm guaranteed to make you rock
I said 1-2-3-4, tell me Wonder Mike, what are you
waitin' for?

[Wonder Mike]
I said-a hip hop, the hippie to the hippie
The hip hip hop, a-you don't stop
The rock it to the bang bang boogie say up
jumped the boogie
To the rhythm of the boogie, the beat
Skiddlee beebop a-we rock a scoobie doo
And guess what America? We love you
Cos ya rock and ya roll with so much soul
You could rock till you're a hundred and one years old
I don't mean to brag, I don't mean to boast
But we like hot butter on our breakfast toast
Rock it up baby bubbah
Baby bubbah to the boogie da bang bang da boogie
To the beat beat, it's so unique
Come on everybody and dance to the beat.

I said-a hip hop the hippie the hippie
To the hip hip hop, a you don't stop
Rock it out baby bubbah to the boogie da bang bang
The boogie to the boogie da beat
I said I can't wait till the end of the week
When I'm rappin' to the rhythm of a groovy beat
And attempt to raise your body heat
Just blow your mind so that you can't speak
And do a thing but a rock and shuffle your feet
And let it change up to a dance called the freak
And when ya finally do come into your rhythmic beat
Rest a little while so ya don't get weak
I know a man named Hank
He has more rhymes than a serious bank
So come on Hank, sing that song
To the rhythm of the boogie da bang bang da bong.

[Big Bank Hank]
Well, I'm imp the dimp the ladies pimp
The women fight for my delight
But I'm the grandmaster with the three MCs
That shock the house for the young ladies
And when you come inside, into the front
You do the freak, spank, and do the bump
And when the sucker MCs try to prove a point
We're treacherous trio, we're the serious joint
From sun to sun and from day to day
I sit down and write a brand new rhyme
Because they say that miracles never cease
I've created a devastating masterpiece
I'm gonna rock the mic till you can't resist
Everybody, I say it goes like this:
Well I was comin' home late one dark afternoon
A reporter stopped me for a interview
She said she's heard stories and she's heard fables
That I'm vicious on the mic and the turntables
This young reporter I did adore
So I rocked a vicious rhyme like I never did before
She said: 'Damn, fly guy, I'm in love with you!'
'The Casanova legend must have been true.'
I said, 'By the way baby what's your name?'
Said, 'I go by the name of Lois Lane.'
'And you could be my boyfriend you surely can
Just let me quit my boyfriend called Superman.'
I said, 'He's a fairy, I do suppose
Flyin' through the air in pantyhose
He may be very sexy or even cute
But he looks like a sucker in a blue and red suit
I said you need a man who's got finesse
And his whole name across his chest
He may be able to fly all through the night
But can he rock a party till the early light?
He can't satisfy you with his little worm
But I can bust you out with my super sperm'
I go do it, I go do it, I go do it, do it, do it
An I'm here an' I'm there, I'm Big Bank Hank,
I'm everywhere
Just throw your hands up in the air
And party hardy like you just don't care
Let's do it don't stop y'all, a tick a tock
y'all you don't stop
Go hotel motel what you gonna do
today (say what?)
I'm gonna get a fly girl
Gonna get some spank, drive off in a def OJ
Everybody go hotel motel Holiday Inn
You say if your girl starts actin' up then
you take her friend
I say skip, dive, what can I say?
I can't fit em all inside my OJ

So I just take half and bust them out
I give the rest to Master Gee so he could
shock the house.

[Master Gee]
It was twelve o'clock one Friday night
I was rockin' to the beat and feelin' all right
Everybody was dancin' on the floor
Doin' all the things they never did before
And then this fly fly girl with a sexy lean
She came into the bar, she came into the scene
As she travelled deeper inside the room
All the fellas checked out her white sasoons
She came up to the table, looked into my eyes
Then she turned around and shook her behind
So I said to myself, it's time for me to release
My vicious rhyme I call my masterpiece
And now people in the house this is just for you
A little rap to make you boogaloo
Now the group ya hear is called Phase Two
And let me tell ya somethin', we're a helluva crew
Once a week we're on the street
Just a-cuttin' the jams and making it free
For you to party, ya got to have the moves
So we'll get right down and give you the groove
For you to dance you gotta get hype
So we'll get right down for you tonight
Now the system's on and the girls are there
Ya definitely have a rockin' affair
But let me tell ya somethin' there's still one fact
That to have a party ya got to have a rap
So when the party's over you're makin' it home
And tryin' to sleep before the break of dawn
And while ya sleepin' ya start to dream
And thinkin' how ya danced on the disco scene
My name appears in your mind
Yeah, a name you know that was right on time
It was Phase Two, just a-doin' a do
Rockin' ya down cause ya know we could
To the rhythm of the beat that makes ya freak
Come alive girls, get on your feet
To the rhythm of the beat to the beat the beat
To the double beat beat that it makes ya freak
To the rhythm of the beat that says ya go on
On-n-on into the break of dawn
Now I got a man comin' on right now
He's guaranteed to throw down
He goes by the name of Wonder Mike
Come on Wonder Mike, do what ya like.

[Wonder Mike]
Like a can of beer that's sweeter than honey
Like a millionaire that has no money
Like a rainy day that is not wet
Like a gamblin' fiend that does not bet
Like Dracula without his fangs
Like the boogie to the boogie without the boogie bang
Like collard greens that don't taste good
Like a tree that's not made out of wood
Like goin' up and not comin' down
Is just like the beat without the sound, no sound
To the beat beat, ya do the freak
Everybody just rock and dance to the beat
Have you ever went over a friend's house to eat
And the food just ain't no good?
I mean the macaroni's soggy, the peas are mushed
And the chicken tastes like wood
So you try to play it off like you think you can
By sayin' that you're full
And then your friend says, momma he's
just being polite
He ain't finished – uh uh, that's bull
So your heart starts pumpin' and you think of a lie
And you say that you already ate
And your friend says man, there's plenty of food
So you pile some more on your plate
While the stinky foods steamin' your mind
starts to dreamin'
Of the moment that it's time to leave
And then you look at your plate and your
chicken's slowly rottin'
Into something that looks like cheese
Oh so you say that's it, I got to leave this place
I don't care what these people think
I'm just sittin' here makin' myself nauseous
With this ugly food that stinks
So you bust out the door while it's still closed
Still sick from the food you ate
And then you run to the store for quick relief
From a bottle of kaopectate
And then you call your friend two weeks later
To see how he has been
And he says I understand about the food
Baby bubbah but we're still friends
With a hip hop the hippie to the hippie
The hip hip a hop a you don't stop the rockin'
To the bang bang boogie
Say up jump the boogie to the rhythm of the
boogie the beat
I say Hank, can ya rock?
Can ya rock to the rhythm that just don't stop?
Can ya hip me to the shoobie doo?

[Big Bank Hank]
I said come on make the people move
I go to the halls and then ring the bell
Because I am the man with the clientele
And if ya ask me why I rock so well
A big bang, I got clientele
And from the time I was only six years old
I never forgot what I was told
It was the best advice that I ever had
It came from my wise dear old dad
He said sit down punk I wanna talk to you
And don't say a word until I'm through
Now there's a time to laugh a time to cry
A time to live and a time to die
A time to break and a time to chill
To act civilised or act real ill
But whatever ya do in your lifetime
Ya never let a MC steal your rhyme
So from sixty six till this very day
I'll always remember what he had to say
So when the sucker MCs try to chump my style
I let them know that I'm versatile
I got style finesse and a little black book
That's filled with rhymes and I know you
wanna look
But there's a thing that separates you from me
And that's called originality
Because my rhymes are on from what you heard
I didn't even bite and not a goddamn word
And I say a little more later on tonight
So the sucker MCs can bite all night
A tick a tock y'all, a beat beat y'all
A let's rock y'all ya don't stop
Ya go hotel motel whatcha gonna do
today (say what?)
Ya say I'm gonna get a fly girl gonna get some
spankin'
Drive off in a def OJ
Everybody go hotel motel Holiday Inn
Ya say if your girl starts actin' up then you
take her friends
A-like that y'all, to the beat y'all
Beat beat y'all, ya don't stop
A Master Gee, am I mellow?

[Master Gee]
It's on you so whatcha gonna do?
Well like Johnny Carson on the Late Show
A like Frankie Croker in stereo
Well like the Bar-Kay's singin' Holy Ghost
The sounds to throw down, they're played the most
It's like my man Captain Sky
Whose name he earned with his Super Sperm
We rock and we don't stop

Get off y'all I'm here to give you whatcha got
To the beat that it makes you freak
And come alive girl get on your feet
A-like a Perry Mason without a case
Like Farrah Fawcett without her face
Like the Bar-Kays on the mic
Like getting' right down for you tonight
Like movin' your body so ya don't know how
Right to the rhythm and throw down
Like comin' alive to the Master Gee
The brother who rocks so viciously
I said the age of one my life begun
At the age of two I was doin' the do
At the age of three it was you and me
Rockin' to the sounds of the Master Gee
At the age of four I was on the floor
Givin' all the freaks what they bargained for
At the age of five I didn't take no jive
With the Master Gee it's all the way live
At the age of six I was a pickin' up sticks
Rappin' to the beat my stick was fixed
At the age of seven I was rockin' in heaven
Don't cha know I went off
I got right on down to the beat you see
Getting' right on down, makin' all the girls
Just take of their clothes to the beat the beat
To the double beat beat that makes you freak
At the age of eight I was really great
Cos every night you see I had a date
At the age of nine I was right on time
Cos every night I had a party rhyme
Goin on-n-n on-n on on-n on
The beat don't stop until the break of dawn
A sayin' on-n-n on-n on on-n on
Like a hot buttered de pop de pop de pop
A saying o-n-n on-n on on-n on
Cos I'm a helluva man when I'm on the mic
I am the definite feast delight
Cos I'm a helluva man when I'm on the mic
I am the definite feast delight
Come to the Master Gee you see
The brother who rocks so viciously.

Music by Bernard Edwards & Nile Rodgers
Words by S. Robinson, H. Jackson, M. Wright & G. O'Brien

SUGARHILL GANG...

Although 'Rapper's Delight' is widely regarded as the first rap single, that accolade truly belongs to the Fatback Band's 'King Tim III (Personality Jock)', the flip to their 'You're My Candy Sweet' single. Still, it does serve as a jumping off point for hip hop's existence on vinyl. Established as a youth cult long before 1979, hip hop was all about parties and jams using cut-up sections of other people's records and improvised battle rhymes. No-one had the financial resources or instinct to record the results. Enter Sylvia Robinson, one-time R&B star and co-founder (with husband Joe) of Sugar Hill Records, who came across the music via her children's mix tapes. She could see its potential and immediately set about exploiting it with the assistance of a few neighbourhood kids.

Wonder Mike (Wright) was a friend of her eldest son, while Guy 'Master Gee' O'Brien was recruited through auditions. The trio was completed by Big Bank Hank (Henry Jackson), a bouncer, pizza shop worker and part-time manager of the Cold Crush Brothers. 'Rapper's Delight', at nearly 17 minutes long, was recorded in a single take and based on Chic's 'Good Times' (recreated in the studio rather than sampled). As Big Bank Hank later recalled: 'One take, no mistakes. Don't stop or stutter. A 17-minute record done in 17 minutes and 50 seconds. When you're hungry, you want to do something right.' Alas, Hank's hunger also led him to 'lift' a series of couplets by his friend and Cold Crush Brother Grandmaster Caz, who'd lent him his book of rhymes.

On release the record took New York by storm, as scene veteran Davy D recalls: 'A lot of cats were happy and in awe to hear a rap record, but at the same time everyone was confused as to who the group was. No-one had ever heard of the Sugarhill Gang. Adding to the confusion were people hearing rhymes that were familiar and easily recognised. That's because Caz had an awesome rep and was real popular... But the bottom line was Sugar Hill had committed three major violations. First they bit [stole] Caz's rhymes. Secondly, they took someone else's name when Hank called himself the Casanova Fly. Finally they used the word rap to describe what we called emceeing. The word rap was never used prior to '79 to describe the technique of rhyming to music on the mic.'

Others were even less enchanted with these New Jersey interlopers. 'What the fuck are they doing with our art form?' reminisced Melle Mel in *The Hip Hop Years*. 'It's like they axe-murdered the shit.'

Regardless of its authenticity or artistic credibility, 'Rapper's Delight' introduced a new paradigm in hip hop music. And its fame spread far beyond New York. When St. Louis station WESL played it for the first time the phone lines were jammed for 12 hours by repeat requests – ironic, given that Joe Robinson had originally considered it too long to be a radio hit. But as Chuck D of Public Enemy once said, 'It wasn't how long the 15 minutes were, but how short the 15 minutes were.'

The Sugarhill Gang enjoyed a few further hits with '8th Wonder' and 'Apache', but were gradually eclipsed by more cutting edge artists in the early 80s. However, the success of 'Rapper's Delight' has enabled them to continue touring to this day. Just don't lend Hank your homework.

KURTIS BLOW...

Born Kurtis Walker in Harlem in the late 50s,
Blow was present at the birth of hip hop as an original
b-boy. 'Break-boys' were named after the youths who
followed DJ Kool Herc's Bronx party jams, improvising
jerky dance movements around the 'breakdown'
passages of the records Herc span. 'I was one of those
b-boy dancers and one of the best in Harlem', Blow
recalled in the sleevenotes to his anthology of old
school rap for Rhino Records: 'I loved to travel up to
the Bronx and battle with the Herculoids (Kool Herc
followers): the Nigga Twins, Clark Kent, D.ST,
DJ Coke La Rock, etc.'.

Studying a communications course during the day,
his nights were spent at venues such as Harlem's
Charles' Gallery, either as a DJ (spinning the records)
or MC (rapping 'shout-outs' to his regulars). His
nocturnal activities led to a friendship with Rush
Management and Def Jam Records' founder Russell
Simmons, a fellow student at the City College Of
New York. After suggesting Blow dispense with his
choice of stage name (he was known as Kool DJ Kurt
in tribute to Kool Herc) he negotiated a deal with
Mercury, making him first rapper to secure a
major label contract.

Recorded in 1980, 'The Breaks' was, according to the
Vibe History of Hip Hop, 'possibly the most pivotal
recording in the whole history of hip hop: the first to
rock b-boys, punkers and new-wavers alike, a
masterful melding of seamlessly-flowing blocks of
rhythm and lyrical double-entendres'. It employed
party atmospherics as a chorus mechanism (with
contributions from famed hip hop author Nelson
George) over its seven minutes and 46 seconds.
Partly inspired by comedian Eddie Lawrence, the
song's protagonist is dogged by claims on his time and
money before reconciling himself to his misfortune.
Or, in the Bronx vernacular adopted from old
American B-movies such as Humphrey Bogart's *Action
In The North Atlantic*, 'dem's da breaks'. Blow's 'Hard
Times' also addressed urban frustrations ('Livin' on
the uptown side of jive/Hustlin' a buck to stay alive').
However, both songs bemoaned the author's ill fortune
rather than examining social policy in any detail.

A massive summer hit in 1980, 'The Breaks' sold half
a million copies and was the first rap 12-inch to be
certified gold. It seemed Blow might emerge as 'the
king of rap' that Simmons billed him as. Ultimately his
career waned as his gimmicky, party-based rhyming
became outmoded with the arrival of hard-hitting acts
like Run-DMC (ironically, acolyte Joseph 'Run'
Simmons once advertised himself as 'the son of Kurtis
Blow'). After the poorly-received and inaccurately-
titled *Back By Popular Demand* in 1988, Blow
concentrated on production, DJ work, TV appearances
and promoting old school rap reunion tours.

Clap your hands, everybody
If you got what it takes
Cos I'm Kurtis Blow and I want you to know
That these are the breaks.

Brakes on a bus, brakes on a car
Breaks to make you a superstar
Breaks to win and breaks to lose
But these here breaks will rock your shoes
And these are the breaks
Break it up, break it up, break it up!

If your woman steps out with another man
(That's the breaks, that's the breaks)
And she runs off with him to Japan
And the IRS says they want to chat
And you can't explain why you claimed your cat

To the girl in brown, stop messing around
(Break it up, break it up)
To the guy in blue, watcha gonna do?
To the girl in green, don't be so mean
And the guy in red, say what I said
Break down!

Brakes on a plane, brakes on a train
Breaks to make you go insane
Breaks in love, breaks in war
But we got the breaks to get you on the floor
And these are the breaks
Break it up, break it up, break it up!
Break down! Yo!

KURTIS BLOW
THE BREAKS (PART 1)
RELEASED 1980: INCLUDED ON KURTIS BLOW (1980)

And Ma Bell sends you a whopping bill
With 18 phone calls to Brazil
And you borrowed money from the mob
And yesterday you lost your job
Well, these are the breaks
Break it up, break it up, break it up.

Throw your hands up in the sky
And wave 'em 'round from side to side
And if you deserve a break tonight
Somebody say all right! (All right)
Say ho-oh! (Ho-oh!)
And you don't stop
Keep on, somebody scream! (Oww!)
Break down!

Breaks on a stage, breaks on a screen
Breaks to make your wallet lean
Breaks run cold and breaks run hot
Some folks got 'em and some have not
But these are the breaks
Break it up, break it up, break it up!
Break down!

Just do it, just do it, just do it, do it, do it!
Just do it, just do it, just do it, do it, do it!
Just do it, just do it, just do it, do it, do it!
Just do it, just do it, just do it, do it, do it!

You say last week you met the perfect guy
(That's the breaks, that's the breaks)
And he promised you the stars in the sky
He said his Cadillac was gold
But he didn't say it was ten years old
He took you out to the Red Coach grill
But he forgot the cash and you paid the bill
And he told you the story of his life
But he forgot the part about . . . his wife!
Huh! Huh!

Well, these are the breaks!
Break it up, break it up, break it up! Break down!

Words & Music by James B. Moore, Robert Ford,
Kurtis Blow, Russell Simmons & Lawrence Smith

It's like a jungle
Sometimes it makes me wonder
How I keep from goin' under (x2).

Broken glass everywhere
People pissin' on the stairs
You know they just don't care
I can't take the smell, can't take the noise
Got no money to move out, I guess I got no choice
Rats in the front room, roaches in the back
Junkies in the alley with a baseball bat
I tried to get away but I couldn't get far
Cos a man with a tow-truck repossessed my car.

Don't push me, cos I'm close to the edge
I'm trying not to lose my head.

It's like a jungle
Sometimes it makes me wonder
How I keep from goin' under.

My brother's doin' bad, stole my mother's TV
Says she watches too much, it's just not healthy
All My Children in the daytime, Dallas at night
Can't even see the game or the Sugar Ray fight
The bill collectors, they ring my phone
And scare my wife when I'm not home
Got a bum education, double-digit inflation
Can't take the train to the job, there's a strike
at the station
Neon King Kong standin' on my back
Can't stop to turn around, broke my sacroiliac
A mid-range migraine, cancered membrane
Sometimes I think I'm goin' insane
I swear I might hijack a plane!

Don't push me, cos I'm close to the edge
I'm trying not to lose my head.

It's like a jungle
Sometimes it makes me wonder
How I keep from goin' under (x2).

GRANDMASTER FLASH
& THE FURIOUS FIVE
THE MESSAGE
RELEASED: 1982. INCLUDED ON: MESSAGE FROM THE BEAT STREET:
THE BEST OF GRANDMASTER FLASH, MELLE MEL & THE FURIOUS FIVE (1994)

Standin' on the front stoop hangin' out the window
Watchin' all the cars go by, roarin' as
the breezes blow
Crazy lady, livin' in a bag
Eatin' outta garbage pails, used to be a fag hag
Said she'll dance the tango, skip the light fandango
A Zircon princess seemed to lost her senses
Down at the peep show watchin' all the creeps
So she can tell her stories to the girls back home
She went to the city and got so so seditty
She had to get a pimp, she couldn't make it
on her own.

Don't push me, cos I'm close to the edge
I'm trying not to lose my head.

It's like a jungle
Sometimes it makes me wonder
How I keep from goin' under (x2).

My son said, Daddy, I don't wanna go to school
Cos the teacher's a jerk, he must think I'm a fool
And all the kids smoke reefer, I think it'd be cheaper
If I just got a job, learned to be a street sweeper
Or dance to the beat, shuffle my feet
Wear a shirt and tie and run with the creeps
Cos it's all about money, ain't a damn thing funny
You got to have a con in this land of
milk and honey
They pushed that girl in front of the train
Took her to the doctor, sewed her
arm on again
Stabbed that man right in his heart
Gave him a transplant for a brand
new start
I can't walk through the park
'cos it's crazy after dark
Keep my hand on my gun
cos they got me on the run
I feel like a outlaw, broke
my last glass jaw

Hear them say 'You want some more.'
Livin' on a see-saw.

Don't push me, cos I'm close to the edge
I'm trying not to lose my head.

Say what?
It's like a jungle
Sometimes it makes me wonder
How I keep from goin' under (x2).

A child is born with no state of mind
Blind to the ways of mankind
God is smilin' on you but he's frownin' too
Because only God knows what you'll go through
You'll grow in the ghetto livin' second-rate

And your eyes will sing a song called deep hate
The places you play and where you stay
Looks like one great big alleyway
You'll admire all the number-book takers
Thugs, pimps and pushers and the big
money-makers
Drivin' big cars, spendin' twenties and tens
And you'll wanna grow up to be just like them
Smugglers, scramblers, burglars, gamblers
Pickpocket peddlers, even panhandlers
You say I'm cool, huh, I'm no fool
But then you wind up droppin' outta high school
Now you're unemployed, all non-void
Walkin' round like you're Pretty Boy Floyd
Turned stick-up kid, but look what you done did
Got sent up for a eight-year bid
Now your manhood is took and you're a Maytag
Spend the next two years as a undercover fag
Bein' used and abused to serve like hell
Till the day you found hung dead in the cell
It was plain to see that your life was lost
You was cold and your body swung
back and forth
But now your eyes sing the sad, sad song
Of how you lived so fast and died so young.

Don't push me, cos I'm close to the edge
I'm trying not to lose my head.

Words & Music by Edward Fletcher, Sylvia Robinson,
Clifton Chase & Melvin Glover

© *Copyright 1982 Sugar Hill Music Publishing Limited, USA.*
IQ Music Limited, Commercial House, 52 Perrymount Road,
Haywards Heath, West Sussex RH16 3DT.
All Rights Reserved. International Copyright Secured.

GRANDMASTER FLASH & THE FURIOUS FIVE

GRANDMASTER FLASH...

This genre-crushing juggernaut, one of the few old school hip hop records that has never dated, is as succinct an expression of urban anxiety as has ever existed in popular music's lexicon. It owes much of its creation not to the titular author Grandmaster Flash, whose role was diminishing just as hip hop evolved from a performance-based medium to a recorded one, but to one Ed Fletcher, a session musician at Sugar Hill Records.

Fletcher (a.k.a. Duke Bootee) had come up with a short musical passage to garnish the opening line: 'It's like a jungle'. He ran it by Sugar Hill's commander in chief Sylvia Robinson. She took the embryonic track to the Furious Five, newly arrived from rival Enjoy Records. They were immediately bemused at the lyric. 'There was nothing in rap like that before except for maybe the Last Poets,' protested Furious Five MC Creole, 'and they were more philosophers.' Hip hop at this stage in its development was party music for impoverished people. It sought to free its consumers from their daily grind, not force the misery of their condition back down their throats. Melle Mel eventually agreed to work on the song, adding a few lines he'd already used on the group's 'Super Rappin'' release on Enjoy.

Bootee constructed the track alongside guitarist Skip McDonald. It was the first major single on the label to dispense with the full Sugar Hill house band, employing synthesized bass and drums instead – it is often forgotten that the single spearheaded a sonic as well as lyrical revolution in hip hop. 'The Message' was released in the summer of 1982. It peaked at number four in the R&B lists and number 62 on the main *Billboard* chart, eventually achieving gold certification. It also managed to reach the UK Top 10. But its impact was far greater than those bare statistics suggest.

Via 'The Message' hip hop not only opened up a dialectic with a new, global audience, but also with itself. Those initially surprised at its subject matter soon succumbed. 'Don't push me, 'cos I'm close to the edge' rivalled the power of any sentiment in popular culture. As Melle Mel pointed out, 'At that time, half the

people in America probably wanted to say that'. Or as hip hop author Nelson George remembers, 'It was sophisticated, powerful social commentary in hip hop and it just hadn't been done before. It spoke very powerfully for what was going on underneath Reagan's America'.

Flash was irritated by his displacement in the pecking order, but rode the crest of the group's popularity along with his former supporting cast of MCs, who were rapidly becoming the star attraction. However, drug consumption and envies ate away at their sense

of purpose. They cut two more great records, Flash's show-stopping DJ odyssey 'The Adventures Of Grandmaster Flash On The Wheels Of Steel' and 'White Lines (Don't Do It)', a semi-autobiographical appraisal of the group's descent into cocaine addiction. But 'The Message' had a profound impact on everyone that followed, from Run-D.M.C. to Public Enemy to today's 'reality rappers'.

[Run]
Two years ago, a friend of mine
Asked me to say some MC rhyme
So I said this rhyme I'm about to say
The rhyme was Def, a-then it went this way
Took a test to become an MC
And Orange Krush became amazed at me
So Larry put me inside his Cadillac
The chauffeur drove off and we never came back
Dave cut the record down to the bone
And now they got me rockin' on the microphone
And then we talkin' autograph, and here's the laugh
Champagne, caviar, and bubble bath
But see, ah that's the life that I lead
And you sucker M.C.s is who I please
So take that and move back, catch a heart attack
Because there's nothin' in the world that
Run'll ever lack
I cold chill at a party in a b-boy stance

You five dollar boy and I'm a million dollar man
You's a sucker MC, and you're my fan
You try to bite lines, but rhymes are mine
You's a sucker MC in a pair of Calvin Klein
Comin' from the wackest part of town
Tryin' to rap up but you can't get down
You don't even know your English, your verb or noun
You're just a sucker MC you sad face clown
So D.M.C. and if you're ready
The people rockin' steady
You're drivin' big cars get your gas from Getti.

[D.M.C.]
I'm D.M.C. in the place to be
I go to St. John's University
And since kindergarten I acquired the knowledge
And after 12th grade I went straight to college
I'm light skinned, I live in Queens
And I love eatin' chicken and collard greens
I dress to kill, I love the style

RUN-D.M.C.

SUCKER M.C.S (KRUSH-GROOVE 1)

RELEASED: 1982. INCLUDED ON: RUN-D.M.C. (1984)

And rock on the mic and make the girls wanna dance
Fly like a dove, that come from up above
I'm rockin' on the mic and you can call me Run-Love.

I got a big long Caddy not like a Seville
And written right on the side it reads 'Dressed to Kill'
So if you see me cruisin' girls just a-move or step aside
There ain't enough room to fit you all in my ride
It's on a first come, first serve basis
Coolin' out girl, take you to the def places
One of a kind and for your people's delight
And for you sucker MC, you just ain't right
Because you're bitin' all your life, you're
cheatin' on your wife
You're walkin' round town like a hoodlum with a knife
You're hangin' on the ave, chillin' with the crew
And everybody know what you've been through.

With the one-two-three, three to two-one
My man Larry Larr, my name DJ Run
We do it in the place with the highs and the bass
I'm rockin' to the rhythm won't you watch it on my face
Go uptown and come down to the ground
You sucker MCs, you bad face clown

I'm an MC you know who's versatile
Say I got good credit in your regards
Got my name not numbers on my credit cards
I go uptown, I come back home with who?
Me myself and my microphone.

All my rhymes are sweet delight
So here's another one for y'all to bite
When I rhyme, I never quit
And if I got a new rhyme I'll just say it
Cos it takes a lot to entertain
And sucker MCs can be a pain
You can't rock a party with the hip in hop
You gotta let 'em know you'll never stop
The rhymes have to make (a lot of sense)·
You got to know where to start (when the
beats commence).

Words & Music by Darryl McDaniels,
Joseph Simmons & Larry Smith
© Copyright 1983 Protoons Incorporated/Rush-Groove, USA.
Warner/Chappell Music Limited, Griffin House,
161 Hammersmith Road, London W6 8BS.
All Rights Reserved. International Copyright Secured.

RUN-D.M.C...

They weren't the originators, but Run-D.M.C. were the great popularisers of rap, keeping hip hop's emphasis on beats and rhyme, but wholly abandoning its reliance on fussy disco rhythms in favour of sparse rock percussion. In so doing, Run-D.M.C. brought the curtain down on the groundbreaking party crews of hip hop's first flowering (including their great heroes the Cold Crush Brothers) and ushered in the 'new school' era.

This sea change was signified not only by acoustics but apparel and attitude. Joseph 'Run' Simmons, Darryl 'D.M.C.' McDaniels and Jason 'Jam Master Jay' Mizell were from the 'burbs of Queens, rather than the birthing grounds of the Bronx. And instead of the excesses of attire that the Furious Five and the Sugarhill Gang indulged in, Run-D.M.C. rapped on stage in the clothes they wore on the street. While this later led to a marketing deal with preferred sneaker vendors Adidas, it also confirmed the seismic shift in rap's trajectory. Street-level authenticity displaced the escapism and Broadway production values that had overtaken the old school crews. In another break from the past, Run's elder brother Russell Simmons, still some way off founding Def Jam Records, christened the group Run-D.M.C. instead of their choice of the more traditional Sure Shot Two. They were mortified.

Simmons Senior clinched a deal with Profile for the princely sum of $25,000. Run-D.M.C.'s first release, 'It's Like That' backed by 'Sucker M.C.s', was unarguably the strongest debut single in rap history. The b-side was based on Orange Krush's 'Action', a record Russell had helped create. Larry Smith, the main man behind Orange Krush and later

Run-D.M.C.'s first producer, was invited to re-construct the backing track, which essentially consisted of a drum track programmed by Russell Simmons (he later called his co-production of 'Sucker M.C.'s' 'the single most creative thing I've ever done').

For all the calibrated gusto of their a-side routines, it was the flipside that radio singled out. On 'Sucker MCs' Run-D.M.C. not only gave b-boys a new anthem and rap lyricists a new cliché to play with, they also managed to harness the intensity of the Cold Crush Brothers mix tapes the Hollis schoolfriends had grown up listening to. As D.M.C. attests, 'Sucker M.C.s' was 'the rawest form in rap, it's almost hypnotising. It's almost drugging, almost like a drug, that feeling... There's just something about it that's timeless - it's not a sound, it's not music, it's the energy. It's a vibe.' The original lyric, incidentally, had been a homage to the search for 'cheeba' — 'Went uptown to buy some black/The shit was not the wack'.

Or as future producer and megafan Rick Rubin remembers it, 'It was one of the first records to reduce to that bare minimum of the beat and the voice, the beat and the rhyme. I remember hearing it in a club. It was just a booming sound and there was nothing like it. That was one of the very first really stripped-down records that laid the groundwork for the rest of hip hop. I think 'Walk This Way' did make Run-D.M.C. a household name. From a historical perspective it's important, but from a hip hop song perspective, 'Sucker M.C.'s' - that's the one.

RUN-D.M.C.

[Run]
Run-D.M.C.... (echoed)
For you – Fresh... (echoed)

[Run]
For all you sucker MCs perpetratin' a fraud
Your rhymes are cold wack and keep the crowd cold lost
You're the kind of guy that girl ignored
I'm drivin' Caddy, you fixin' a Ford
My name is Joseph Simmons but my middle name's Lord
And when I'm rockin' on the mic, you
should all applaud
Because we're (wheelin', dealin', we got a funny feelin')
We rock from the floor up to the ceilin'
We groove it (you move it) it has been proven
We calmed the seven seas because our music is soothin'
We create it (relate it) and often demonstrate it
We'll diss a sucker MC make the other suckers hate it
We're rising (suprising) and often hypnotising

[D.M.C.]
So listen to this because it can't be missed
And you can't leave till you're dismissed
You can do anything that you want to
But you can't leave until we're through
So relax your (body) and your mind
And listen to us say this rhyme
(Hey!) You might think that you have (waited)
Long enough till the rhyme was (stated)
But if it were a test it would be (graded)
With a grade that's not (debated)
Nothing too deep and nothing dense
And all our rhymes make a lot of (sense).

RUN-D.M.C.
ROCK BOX
RELEASED: 1984. INCLUDED ON: RUN-D.M.C. (1984)

We always tell the truth and then we never
slip no lies in
No curls (no braids) peasy-head and still get paid
Jam Master cut the record up and down
and cross-fade.

[Run]
Because the rhymes I say, sharp as a nail
Witty as can be and not for sale
Always funky fresh, could never be stale.

[D.M.C.]
Took a test to become an MC and didn't fail
I couldn't wait to demonstrate
All the super def rhymes that I create
I'm a wizard of a word, that's what you heard
And anything else is quite absurd
I'm the master of a mic, that's what I say
And if I didn't say that, you'd say it anyway.

[Run]
Bust into the party, come in the place
See the first things come, the music in your face
Tear down the walls, some of the floor
With the DJ named Jay with the cuts galore.

[Together]
So move your butt, to the cut
Run amuk, you're not in a rut
Each and everybody out there, we got the notion.
[D.M.C.]
We want to see y'all all in motion.

[Together]
Just shake, wiggle, jump up and down
Move your body to the funky sound.

[D.M.C.]
Side to side, back and forth

[Together]
We're the two MCs, and we're gonna go off
Stand in place, walk or run
Tap your feet, you'll be on the one.

[D.M.C.]
Just snap your fingers and clap your hands.

[TOGETHER]
Our DJ's better than all these bands
Huh!

[Run]
We got all the lines
[D.M.C.]
And all the rhymes
[Run]
We don't drop dimes
[D.M.C.]
And we don't do crimes
[Run]
We bake a little cake with Duncan Hines
[D.M.C.]
And never wear the vest they call the Calvin Kleins
[Run]
Cos Calvin Klein's no friend of mine
Don't want nobody's name on my behind
Lee on my legs, sneakers on my feet
D by my side and Jay with the beat.

Ad libs to fade

Words & Music by Darryl McDaniels,
Joseph Simmons & Larry Smith
© Copyright 1984 Protoons Incorporated/Rush-Groove, USA.
Warner/Chappell Music Limited, Griffin House,
161 Hammersmith Road, London W6 8BS.
All Rights Reserved. International Copyright Secured.

RUN-D.M.C...

This is the first instalment in a triumvirate of Run-D.M.C. attempts at rap-rock fusion. It continues through 'King Of Rock', the title-track of their second album, and ends with their fabulous MTV-gatecrashing Aerosmith duel, 'Walk This Way'.

'Rock Box' offered a first glimpse of rappers strutting their stuff over something as trad-rock as a wailing guitar coda. It is also the best early example of the blunt power of Run-D.M.C.'s tag-team raps, a fact that is often overlooked. The interlocking volleys passing between Run and D.M.C., who often finished each other's sentences, established a signature style which dominated rap for the next five years.

When Run-D.M.C. started out they were using 'Good Times' and 'Funky Drummer' as backing tracks just like every other hip hop act going. Indeed, 'Rock Box' wasn't originally conceived as a 'rock' record. Its origins lay in a breakbeat favourite – Otis Redding and Carla Thomas's 1967 Stax oldie 'Tramp'. As D.M.C. remembers, '"Rock Box" was actually gonna be "Tramp", 'cos you could really just flow on that. I came up with the beat, Larry [Smith] put the bass line on it. I went in there we said we're gonna do it, me and Run gonna switch off, back and forth lyrics, and then we're just gonna freestyle. And that record was basically a freestyle session. So we did that and then added the bass line on it. Cool.'

Simmons Snr then roped in session guitarist Eddie Martinez in an attempt to convince MTV that 'rappers could rock'. Not that his younger brother and D.M.C. knew anything about it. 'We get back to the studio,' recalls D.M.C. 'and they got these loud rock guitars on the record!' The twin MCs had come round to the idea of co-opting rock beats, but the formula had always been to take the intros *before* the singing or guitar track came in, rather than allow the two idioms to co-exist. 'These guys got their rock guitars playing through the whole record!' remembers a shocked D.M.C.

He and Run were petrified in case their b-boy fans dismissed the results. Eventually they gained a concession – there should be alternate guitar and guitar-free versions. 'Gave it to radio, what does radio do? Play the version with the guitars going all way through the record,' sighs D.M.C. But the b-boys loved it, so that was OK.

RUN-D.M.C.

LL COOL J...

As hip hop bloomed in the mid-80s, James Todd Smith offered the defining image of the well-heeled rapper – suave, iceberg-cool, his centre of gravity reduced by the sheer weight of gold dangling from his bare torso. However, this persona was an act born of an impossibly shy youth. Indeed, his stage name LL Cool J – or Ladies Love Cool James – was adopted in hope rather than expectation of any success with the opposite sex.

He'd been rhyming since the age of nine, mixing and cutting tapes on decks purchased by his grandfather. These DIY efforts were mailed to everyone he could think of. The only responsive ears belonged to Rick Rubin, in the process of setting up a record label in his university dorm. In 1984 Def Jam released his first single, 'I Need A Beat', which sold 100,000 copies and established his reputation as an incisive, street-smart lyricist. Abandoning his studies, in 1985 LL cut his platinum-selling debut album *Radio*. Thereafter he became the most photogenic, personable rapper of his generation, though he often ditched quality control in pursuit of raw charm. Follow-up album *Bigger And Deffer* alienated former advocates due to the inclusion of slushy ballad-rap, 'I Need Love', as he now openly courted pop audiences. He was a massive hit with the ladies, embarking on a life of sexual conquest in belated justification of his stage name.

'I Can't Live Without My Radio' celebrates a 16-year-old b-boy's most prized possession, his beatbox, and his refusal to compromise on the volume with which he terrorises the neighbourhood. LL's description of himself as a hip hop gangster has been suggested as a precursor to the breakthrough of NWA and their gun-toting ilk, though in reality it is a further manifestation of the cartoon bragging and dissing which characterised early rap records – and of which LL Cool J was, for some time, the master.

The urgent, declamatory rhymes were accompanied by typical Rick Rubin production – stripped-down, metronomic beats, nothing fancy, nothing wasted. A 90-second clip of LL freestyling 'I Can't Live Without My Radio' was featured in the rap rat pack movie *Krush Groove*, which was the closest the song came to a promotional video. It subsequently became a hit on the US R&B charts in its own right, peaking at number 15.

My radio, believe me, I like it loud
I'm the man with a box that can rock the crowd
Walking down the street, to the hardcore beat
While my JVC vibrates the concrete.

I'm sorry if you can't understand
But I need a radio inside my hand
Don't mean to offend other citizens
But I kick my volume way past ten.

My story is rough, my neighbourhood is tough
But I still sport gold, and I'm out to crush
My name is Cool J, I devastate the show
But I couldn't survive without my radio.

Terrorising my neighbours with the heavy bass
I keep the suckers in fear by the look on my face
My radio's bad from the Boulevard
I'm a hip-hop gangster and my name is Todd.
Just stimulated by the beat, bust out the rhyme
Get fresh batteries if it won't rewind
Cos I play every day, even on the subway
I would have got a summons but I ran away
I'm the leader of the show, keepin' you on the go
But I know I can't live without my radio.

Suckers on my jock when I walk down the block
I really don't care if you're jealous or not
Cos I make the songs, you sing along
And your radio's def when my record's on.

So get off the wall, become involved
All your radio problems have now been solved
My treacherous beats make ya ears respond
And my radio's loud like a fire alarm.

The floor vibrates, the walls cave in
The bass makes my eardrums seem thin
Def sounds in my ride, yes the front and back
You would think it was a party, not a Cadillac.

Cos I drive up to the ave, with the windows closed
And my bass is so loud, it could rip your clothes
My stereo's thumpin' like a savage beast
The level on my power meter will not decrease.
Suckers get mad, cos the girlies scream
And I'm still gettin' paid while you look at me mean
I'm the leader of the show, keepin' you on the go
But I know I can't live without my radio.

I'm the leader of the show, keepin' you on the go
And I know I can't live without my radio.

Don't touch that dial, I'll be upset
Might go into a fit and rip off your neck
Cos the radio's thumpin' when I'm down to play
I'm the royal chief rocker - LL Cool J!

Let your big butt bounce from right to left
Cos it's a actual fact this jam is def
Most definitely created by me

Goin' down in radio history.
I'm good to go on your radio
And I'm cold gettin' paid, cos Rick said so
Make the woofers wallop and your tweeters twitch
Some jealous knuckleheads might try to diss.

But it's nuthin', ya frontin', ya girl I am stuntin'
And my radio's loud enough to keep you gruntin'.

See people can't stop me, neither can the police
I'm a musical maniac to say the least
For you and your radio I made this for

Cool J's here to devastate once more.
Pullin' all the girls, takin' out MCs
If ya try to disrespect me, I just say - please!
Here to command the hip-hop land
Kick it live with a box inside my hand.

I'm the leader of the show, keepin' you on the go
But I know I can't live without my radio.

Farmers Boulevard. Yeah? You know that's
where me and E hang out
Cool out, you know what I'm sayin'?
That's where the crib's at.

LL COOL J
I CAN'T LIVE WITHOUT MY RADIO
RELEASED 1985: INCLUDED ON RADIO (1985)

LL COOL J

My name is Cool J, I'm from the rock
Circulating through your radio non-stop
I'm lookin' at the wires behind the cassette
And now I'm on the right, standing on the eject.

Wearin' light blue Pumas, a whole lotta gold
And jams like these keep me in control
I'm the leader of the show, keepin' you on the go
And I know I can't live without my radio.

Your energy level starts to increase
As my big beat is slowly released
I'm on the radio and at the jam
LL Cool J is who I am.

I'm gonna make ya dance, boogie down and rock
And you'll scratch and shake to my musical plot
And to expand my musical plan
Cut Creator - rock the beat with your hands!

That's right, so don't try to front the move
As you become motivated by the funky groove
You can see me and Earl chillin' on the block
With my box cold kickin' with the gangster rock

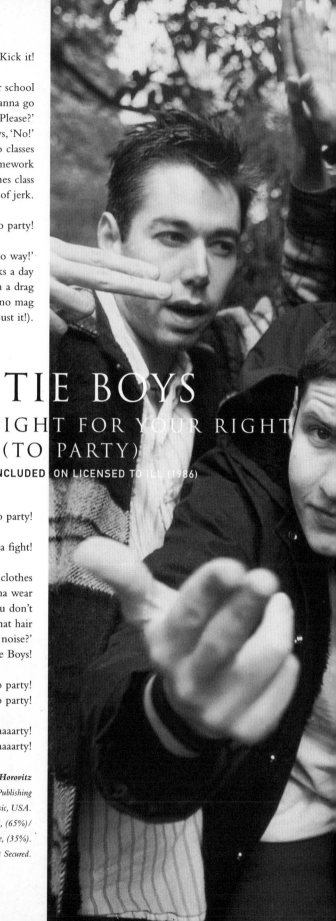

Kick it!

You wake up late for school
Man, you don't wanna go
You ask you mom, 'Please?'
But she still says, 'No!'
You missed two classes
And no homework
But your teacher preaches class
Like you're some kind of jerk.

You gotta fight for your right... To party!

You pop caught you smoking and he said, 'No way!'
That hypocrite smokes two packs a day
Man, living at home is such a drag
Now your mom threw away your best porno mag
(Bust it!).

BEASTIE BOYS
(YOU GOTTA) FIGHT FOR YOUR RIGHT
(TO PARTY)

RELEASED 1986: INCLUDED ON LICENSED TO ILL (1986)

You gotta fight for your right... To party!

You gotta fight!

Don't step out of this house if that's the clothes
you're gonna wear
I'll kick you out of my home if you don't
cut that hair
Your mom busted in and said, 'What's that noise?'
Aw, mom you're just jealous – it's the Beastie Boys!

You gotta fight for your right... To party!
You gotta fight for your right... To party!

Paaaaaaaaaaaaaaaaarty!
Paaaaaaaaaaaaaaaaarty!

BEASTIE BOYS...

Obnoxious pasty-skinned b-boys turned kings of New York cool, the Beastie Boys have carved their initials deep into the bark of rock, pop and hip hop history.

It's no surprise that their offering is the shortest lyric in this book by a country mile. It's not their most erudite effort either, but it is certainly their most zeitgeist-grabbing. Indeed, for many not truly versed in the ways of the Beasties, it's probably all they remember, alongside the tabloid headlines and Volkswagen pendants. It's not hard to see why the song made such a strong connection with the international unwashed. If there's one thing that's universal about the teenage experience it's kicking up a racket and moaning about yer folks. That the Beastie Boys combined both elements in this generational groundhog day of a rap was a stroke of genius. It's a song that's 99% attitude, steeped in locker room bravado and backed by a coruscating Rick Rubin production that betrays his heavy metal roots. In fact, it was the final track recorded for debut album *Licensed To Ill*, satisfying Rubin's desire for an 'anthem'.

It's hard to imagine just how at odds the trio of Ad-Rock (Adam Horovitz), MCA (Adam Yauch) and Mike D (Michael Diamond) seemed at the outset. Most execs were a little ill at ease trying to sell rap, period. Where the market was for a suburban Jewish hip hop group was anyone's guess. Fortunately, Columbia had just signed a distribution deal with Def Jam that helped put some marketing muscle behind the Beastie Boys (though LL Cool J was definitely the priority act). 'Fight For Your Right' rocketed their debut album to double platinum status within two months of release – and its creators to international notoriety as the gutter press tried to turn them into post-Pistols-pariahs (even inventing a story about them abusing terminally-ill kids).

Thereafter the Beasties have pursued an artistic policy encompassing whimsicality, splatter-gun psychedelia, fist-funk adventurism and acerbic, contrary social commentary. Never has the grass grown under them, even if they've ingested quite a bit in the process. Each of their subsequent albums has provided further evidence that the Beastie Boys are as good at hijacking a beat as anyone, employing them with intelligence and flair. 'Fight For Your Right' is hardly a representative selection, but it remains their landmark single.

ERIC B & RAKIM...

'Eric B Is President' was the first track recorded by Eric Barrier and MC William 'Rakim' Griffin, the duo who provided the final punctuation to the new school hip hop aesthetic established by Run-D.M.C. and LL Cool J. It all began when Barrier, an established mobile disc jockey, launched his search for 'New York's top MC' while working for radio station WBLS. In Rakim he not only turned up Long Island's best kept secret, he also found arguably the greatest MC and lyricist in rap.

Barrier's former room-mate and Juice Crew founder Marley Marl had just engendered his own paradigm shift in hip hop by accidentally sampling a James Brown snare. Eric pestered him into giving him time at his home studio on 12th Street. He knew an MC from Long Island who might sound 'nice'. But when first-choice MC Freddie Foxxx declined, Barrier introduced Rakim. Marley Marl was immediately won over by Rakim's calm but steely delivery. But he had reservations. The first demo of 'Eric B Is President' they cut was a pedestrian 80bpm. So Marley Marl introduced them to a rhythm track he had been working on. 'I used to have samples of my drum sounds of the week,' he recalls. 'Every song I produced would have those same drum sounds for the week, then I'll go to another drum sound for the next week. So you could tell the week that I made

"Eric B For President". "The Bridge" [by MC Shan, his classic celebration of Queensbridge life] and all that was done the same week. Because it was still fresh in the sampler and I just tapped out a new pattern for every new record.'

The track was cut on a Tuesday and Marley Marl thought no more about it. On the following Saturday, to his exasperation, he heard it on the radio. 'Why is it on the radio? We didn't even mix the record. We just made a little demo copy that goes all over the place, vocals loud and low, drums clipping in. Next thing I know, Eric comes back with wax. He's like: "You! Hey, here's that joint". I'm like: "Oh, you mastered it off a *cassette*?".' But while Marley Marl was flummoxed by the technical limitations of the recording process now embedded in the final version of the track, Eric B simply insisted that the 'vibe is hot'. He may not have been president in reality, but unlike so many real-life presidents, Eric B knew exactly what he was doing.

What Marley hadn't realised was that the rough mix added rather than detracted from the finished cut. And in Rakim, whose complex rhymes were informed by the wise-guy prison creed of the Five Per Cent Nation (basic tenet: only five per cent of the population reach true enlightenment, the rest are scrabbling around in the intellectual and spiritual quagmire), it introduced a rapper who was so comfortable at the microphone, it sounded as if he'd suckled on it as an infant.

As Marley Marl confirms, 'Eric B Is President' endures as a hip hop staple. 'You could throw it on at any party and at any point and as soon as people hear it they're losing it. That's a classic moment.'

I came in the door, I said it before
I never let the mic magnetise me no more
But it's biting me, fighting me, inviting me to rhyme
I can't hold it back, I'm looking for the line
Taking off my coat, clearing my throat
My rhyme will be kicking it until I hit my last note
My mind'll range to find all kinds of ideas
Self-esteem makes it seem like a thought took
years to build
But still say a rhyme after the next one
Prepared, never scared, I'll just bless one
And you know that I'm the soloist
So Eric B, make 'em clap to this.

I don't bug out or chill or be acting ill
No tricks in '86, it's time to build
Eric B – easy on the cut, no mistakes allowed
Cuz to me, MC means move the crowd
I made it easy to dance to this

ERIC B & RAKIM
ERIC B IS PRESIDENT
RELEASED: 1986. INCLUDED ON: PAID IN FULL (1987)

ERIC B & RAKIM

But can you detect what's coming next from the
flex of the wrist
Saying indeed that I precede cuz my man
made a mix
If he bleed he won't need no band-aid to fix
If they can get some around until there's no
rhymes left
I hurry up because the cut will make 'em bleed
to death
But he's kicking it because it ain't no half-stepping
The party is live, the rhyme can't be kept in-
Side, it needs erupting just like a volcano
It ain't the everyday style of the same old rhyme
Because I'm better then the rest of them
Eric B is on the cut and my name is Rakim.

Go get a girl and get soft and warm
Don't get excited, you've been invited to
a quiet storm
But now it's out of hand cuz you told me
you hate me
And then you ask what have I done lately
First you said all you want is love and affection
Let me be your angel and I'll be your protection

Take you out, buy you all kinds of things
I must of got you too hot and burned off
your wings
You caught an attitude, you need food to eat up
I'm scheming like I'm dreaming on a couch
wit' my feet up
You scream I'm lazy, you must be crazy
Thought I was a donut, you tried to glaze me.

Funky...

It was Saturday night and I'm feelin' kinda sporty
Went to the bar, caught me a 40
Got kinda high and kinda drunk
So I kicked the ass of this little punk
Forgot my key and had to ring my bell
My momma came dressed, she said, 'Who the hell?'
Wait Momma, wait, it's me, ya little son
Before I knew it, my mom pulled a gun
'I know who you are, but who the hell is that?'
I turned around, man, this bitch was fat
I really don't know, she got into the car
I musta picked her up when I left the bar
Ya know I'm horny homey man, I wanted to chill
But you know how mothers are, she wanted to ill
So I said, 'Hey baby, is you on the pill?
'Cos, tonight I wanna be your lover
Just one thing: I forgot to buy a rubber'
Wait a little while then we snuck upstairs
Step by step with a hint of fear
We got into my room, bitch started to scream
Momma busted in with a fucked up scene!

Shirt ripped off, drawers down to my knees
Wait Momma, wait Momma, wait, wait, please!
Put back your gun, put down your brew
My mom fucked up the room
The bitch jumped up with no respect
I had to put the big, big bitch in check
I said, 'Ya come a little closer and ya will get shot,
I'm sober anyway, I don't need no cock'

Oh yeah, them wild Saturday Nights, man...
Know what I mean? They wild as shit, man
They wild, man, ya know?

Yeah, man, let me tell you about
Another Saturday night experience I had...

It was Saturday Night and I was feelin' kinda funny
Gold around my neck, pockets full of money
Went to the corner, man who did I see?
But the super bad bitch lookin' back at me
I said, 'Fly lady, you got a big butt'

SCHOOLLY D
SATURDAY NIGHT
RELEASED 1987: INCLUDED ON SATURDAY NIGHT: THE ALBUM (1987)

Bitch turned around, all she said was, 'What?'
I said, 'My name is Schoolly baby, I'm down
with the Shores'
Before I knew it up came my boys
Noisy as hell and drunk as shit
Sayin', 'Yo Schoolly Schooll, what time is it?'
Looked a little closer and I knew it was a gag
What I thought was a girl was nothin' but a fag.

Oh, man, ya know what I mean?
It's them wild Saturday nights, man.

I got something else to say, man,
Everybody, it's like this...

Everybody rappin' but they don't know how
Shoulda seen the boy rappin' to the cow
He rapped so hard that the nigga saw smoke
He lit up his cheeba and they both took
a toke
The cow got high and the boy got by
Just don't come in my face and ask me why.

Cheeba Cheeba, ya'll
Yeah it's that cheeba cheeba makin 'em feel like that
Cheeba Cheeba, ya'll.

Some call it Cheeba, some call it weed
It's the killer, it's the filler, it's the thing
that you need
Said Cheeba, Cheeba, y'all.

Little Miss Muffet sat on a tuffet
Smokin a J and scratchin' the itch
Along came a spider and sat down beside her
And said, 'Yo, what's up with that, bitch?'
But then down the road came Mary and her lambs
Smokin' a Lacy in each and every hand
The poor little spider, he couldn't score any
They were two dollar bitches and he only
had a penny.

Cheeba Cheeba, ya'll
Yeah, Cheeba Cheeba, ya'll.

Let me tell ya a little tale about Peter the Pimp
Sucker MC'd, tried to cop a limp
Rode around town in a couple of cars
Got gagged by the man tryin' to stick up a bar
The judge said, 'Boy, what was on your mind?'
He said, 'I had some Cheeba Cheeba, cocaine
and some wine'
The judge said, 'Boy, relax and have a beer
You won't be doin' shit for the next ten years'.

Cheeba Cheeba, ya'll
Yeah, it's that Cheeba Cheeba
Cheeba Cheeba, y'all.

Some call it Cheeba, some call it weed
It's the killer, it's the filler, it's the thing
that you need
So Cheeba Cheeba, ya'll.

Me and my man Code Money, my man M+M
We're just chilling, know what I mean
Happens to be Schoolly D, if you didn't
guess by now
Only Schoolly D makes crazy-ass shit like this.

I give back,
Take it away, Code!

SCHOOLLY D...

In 1987 Jesse Weaver started flipping 'reality rhymes' as a reflection of his own experiences on the streets of America's 'city of brotherly love', Philadelphia. Only his streets were the home of fraternal emnities, score-settling, drug-scoring and woman-baiting. Though he didn't know it at the time he was opening doors that half the population of America's west coast would steam through in an effort to proclaim themselves 'original gangsters' too. His minimalist classic 'P.S.K. (What Does It Mean?)' documented his time running with local hoodlums the Parkside Killers. With his distinctive phraseology (you axe for something, not ask for it) conveying uncomfortable reportage from the front line, there was something arresting about Schoolly's tales long before the ghetto fabulous tradition of modern gangsta rap had been established. Admittedly, there were limitations to his oeuvre, his MCing skills and subject matter. Still, DJ Code Money's echoing fusillade of beats and scratches, as close an approximation of rhythmic gunfire anyone had heard until N.W.A. hit their stride, was grimly compelling.

The gist of 'Saturday Night' is the type of 'sex story' Ice-T later turned his hand to, albeit with more dexterity and wit. It's also notable for being one of the first hardcore rap tracks to espouse drug use – though being a cheerleader for cheeba would be commonplace by the early 90s. There's something deeply schizophrenic about the song's construction which helps to frame its place in hip hop's timeline. Despite the savagery of its subject matter, Schoolly's rap harks back to the innocence of original hip hop party jams by employing a George Clinton-influenced nursery rhyme sequence, albeit with the addition of a little mandatory cursing.

Along with 'P.S.K', 'Put Your Filas On' and 'Gucci Time', 'Saturday Night' is one of four Schoolly D efforts that laid down the foundations of the embryonic hardcore rap movement. Afterwards he lost visibility quickly, drowning under the tidal wave of reality-rappers he'd inspired, and albums such as *How A Black Man Feels* (1991), *Welcome To America* (1994) and *Reservoir Dog* (1995) were tired attempts at keeping pace with the new breed. Touchingly, Schoolly D's 'legendary' stature also diminished when a number of those who'd met him insisted he was a straight-up, sweet kind of guy.

[Reverend Jesse Jackson]
Brothers and sisters,
Brothers and sisters,
I don't know what this world is coming to!

[Chuck D]
Yes – the rhythm, the rebel
Without a pause – I'm lowering my level
The hard rhymer – where you never been I'm in
You want stylin' – you know it's time again
D the enemy – tellin' you to hear it
They praised the music – this time they
play the lyrics
Some say no to the album, the show
Bum rush the sound I made a year ago
I guess you know – you guess I'm just a radical

From a rebel it's final on black vinyl
Soul, rock and roll comin' like a rhino
Tables turn – suckers burn to learn
They can't dis-able the power of my label
Def Jam – tells you who I am
The enemy's public – they really give a damn
Strong Island – where I got 'em wild and
That's the reason they're claimin' that I'm violent
Never silent – no dope gettin' dumb nope
Claimin' where we get our rhythm from
Number one – we hit ya and we give ya some
No gun – and still never on the run
You wanna be an S.1. – Griff will tell you when

PUBLIC ENEMY
REBEL WITHOUT A PAUSE
RELEASED: 1987. INCLUDED ON: IT TAKES A NATION OF MILLIONS TO HOLD US BACK (1988)

Not on sabbatical – yes to make it critical
The only part your body should be partying to
Panther power on the hour from the rebel to you.

Radio – suckers never play me
On the mix – they just OK me
Now known and grown when they're clocking my
zone – it's known
Snakin' and takin' everything that a brother owns
[Hard] – my calling card
Recorded and ordered – supporter of Chesimard
Loud and proud kickin' live next poet supreme
Loop a troop, bazooka, the scheme
[Flavor] – a rebel in his own mind
Supporter of my rhyme
Designed to scatter a line of suckers
Who claim I do crime
They on my time, dig it!

Terminator X (x3)
Terminate it!

And then you'll come again – you'll know
what time it is
Impeach the president – pullin' out the ray-gun
Zap the next one – I could be your Sho-gun
[Suckers] – Don't last a minute
Soft and smooth – I ain't with it
[Hardcore] – rawbone like a razor
I'm like a lazer – I just won't graze ya
Old enough to raise ya – so this will faze ya
Get it right boy and maybe I will praise ya
Playin' the role, I got soul too
Voice my opinion with volume
[Smooth] – not what I am
[Rough] – cos I'm the man.

No matter what the name – we're all the same
Pieces in one big chess game
[Yeah] – the voice of power
Is in the house – go take a shower boy

P.E. a group, a crew – not singular
We wear black Wranglers
We're rap stranglers
You can't angle us
I know you're listenin'
I caught you pissin' in your pants –
You're scared of dissin' us
The crowd is missin' us
We're on a mission y'all.

Terminator X (x3)
Terminator, c'mon!

Attitude – when I'm on fire
Juice on the loose – electric wire
Simple and plain – give me the lane

I'll throw it down your throat like Barkley
See my car keys – you'll never get these
They belong to the 98 posse
You want some more, son? – you wanna get some
Rush the door of a store – pick up the album
You know the rhythm, the rhyme plus the
beat is designed
So I can enter your mind, boys
Bring the noise – my time
Step aside for the flex – Terminator X.

PUBLIC ENEMY...

Public Enemy – the black Sex Pistols or the black
CNN, choose your own cliché – came about as much
by accident as design. Carlton Ridenhour, aka Chuck D,
had been messing about with radio and parties as
part of Long Island's Spectrum City collective, before
co-opting the title of their early composition 'Public
Enemy No. 1'. Rick Rubin at Def Jam heard the song
via D.M.C. of Run-D.M.C. and promptly decided that the
MC on the tape should be his next signing.

Chuck, believing he was far too old to be successful
in an art form then dominated by teen heart-throb
LL Cool J, refused. So Rubin embarked on a campaign
to persuade him, including daily phone calls. Chuck
eventually relented. But Rubin wasn't getting a rapper,
as he envisaged, he was getting a complete package.
Inspired by the old school dynamics of the Furious
Five, Public Enemy would additionally consist of
producer Hank Shocklee, DJ Terminator X, madcap
MC Flavor Flav (whose asides to Chuck D are not part
of the body lyric itself and therefore are not included)
and Professor Griff, intimidating head of the Security

of the First World (think Hot Gossip in combat fatigues). Chuck, Hank, brother Keith Shocklee and Eric 'Vietnam' Sadler set about constructing musical vistas which gave 60s soul music an angry twist and incorporated a political ideology largely forgotten since the civil rights movement that Marvin Gaye, James Brown *et al* soundtracked. The music had to pass a simple test – if Chuck's girlfriend liked it, then it was binned for being too 'soft'. Public Enemy were militant black rock 'n' roll, rather than slick R&B (or 'soul, rock 'n' roll, comin' like a rhino' to borrow from the lyric). This sonic machismo informed much of Public Enemy's subsequent oeuvre and was both a source of strength and weakness (at times the vitality of the message was diluted by offending what should have been natural allies).

Debut album *Yo! Bum Rush The Show* only hinted at the carnage about to be wrought with popular music conventions. *It Takes A Nation Of Millions To Hold Us*

Back broke the dam. One of the most axiomatic albums of the late 20th century, power sparked and fizzed from the grooves of 'Bring The Noise', 'She Watch Channel Zero?!' and their Beastie Boys inversion, 'Party For Your Right To Fight'. But 'Rebel Without A Pause', with its knotted mesh of samples from the JB All-Stars and Miles Davis, founded the pulpit from which Chuck D would make his entrance as rap orator (following a sample of the Reverend Jesse Jackson). As he cleared his throat he took aim at his former detractors – the opening stanza is a direct reaction to opinions voiced at the time of their debut album that Public Enemy's music was fine, but what the hell did the rapper sound like?

Prior to Chuck, the art of MCing was about 'getting nice' on the mic. Chuck's fire and brimstone harangues upped the ante, while Flav added his jester's squawk, or 'treble' to Chuck's 'bass', to paraphrase the album's sleevenotes. And the lyrics were precision-guided. Where 'The Message' had tackled deprivation in oblique terms, Chuck always named names, pointing his finger right into the chest of white corporate America. Among the targets were those pulling the strings behind black radio, which still refused to endorse hip hop.

Meanwhile the Bomb Squad (the name was only adopted in 1990) were doing equally revolutionary things with sound. As Rick Rubin remembers, 'The musical production [framed around James Brown's 'The Funky Drummer'] was really hyped up and chaotic, and so much of the Def Jam sound had been slow and low. Not about uptempo chaos and not about changing beats, but about jamming around one beat. That was a very explosive change from a musical standpoint.' The saxophone-siren break at the song's opening seemed to announce the new order for hip hop, such was the distance – acoustically, thematically, politically – it put between itself and its forerunners.

Recently voted the greatest single of the last 25 years in a poll conducted by *Uncut* magazine, 'Rebel Without A Pause' was actually originally released as the b-side (or 'f-side') to 'You're Gonna Get Yours', the final single to be lifted from *Yo! Bum Rush The Show*. As such it was the first track to be recorded for *It Takes A Nation Of Millions*, becoming the pivotal song on arguably the most important record of the late 80s.

What we need is awareness, we can't get careless
You say what is this? My beloved let's get
down to business
Mental self defensive fitness
(Yo) bum rush the show
You gotta go for what you know
Make everybody see, in order to fight the
powers that be.

Lemme hear you say – Fight the Power (repeat)
We got to fight the powers that be.

Fight the power
We got to fight the powers that be.

Elvis was a hero to most (x3) but he never
meant shit to me
You see straight-up racist that sucker was
Simple and plain
Motherfuck him and John Wayne

1989 the number – another summer (get down)
Sound of the funky drummer
Music hittin' your heart cos I know you got soul

PUBLIC ENEMY
FIGHT THE POWER
RELEASED: 1989. INCLUDED ON: FEAR OF A BLACK PLANET (1990)

(Brothers and sisters, hey)
Listen if you're missin' y'all
Swingin' while I'm singin'
Givin' whatcha gettin'
Knowin' what I know
While the Black bands sweatin'
And the rhythm rhymes rollin'
Got to give us what we want
Gotta give us what we need
Our freedom of speech is freedom or death
We got to fight the powers that be.

Lemme hear you say – Fight the power!

As the rhythm designed to bounce
What counts is that the rhymes
Designed to fill your mind
Now that you've realised the pride's arrived
We got to pump the stuff to make us tough from
the heart
It's a start, a work of art
To revolutionise, make a change, nothin's strange
People, people we are the same
No we're not the same
Cos we don't know the game

Cos I'm black and I'm proud
I'm ready and hyped plus I'm amped
Most of my heroes don't appear on no stamps
Sample a look back you look and find
Nothing but rednecks for 400 years if you check
Don't worry be happy was a number one jam
Damn if I say it you can slap me right here (Get it)
Let's get this party started right
Right on, c'mon
What we got to say –
Power to the people no delay
To make everybody see in order to fight the powers
that be (Fight the Power).

Fight the power
We've got to fight the powers that be.

Words & Music by Carl Ridenhour, Keith Shocklee & Eric Sadler
© Copyright 1989 Def American Songs Incorporated/Your Mother's
Music Incorporated/Reach Music International Incorporated, USA.
Universal Music Publishing Limited, Elsinore House, 77 Fulham
Palace Road, London W6 8JA (62.5%)/Hammer Musik Limited,
Onward House, 11 Uxbridge Street, London W8 7TQ (37.5%).
All Rights Reserved. International Copyright Secured.

PUBLIC ENEMY...

Spike Lee's movie *Do The Right Thing* was a skilful dissection of inner city tensions, which gained a lot of its impetus from this blistering song, memorably deployed in the opening sequence alongside a gyrating Rosie Perez. Lee had contacted Public Enemy's aide Bill Stephney to request a contribution to the project. Lee's intention was to dramatise the resentments festering in Brooklyn, based on real life incidents including the Bernhard Goetz shooting and the death of Eleanor Bumpers (an elderly black lady who died after being 'restrained' by police). Chuck promised that after he returned from European touring commitments with Run-D.M.C., Lee would have his song.

Chuck finished the draft lyric while flying between touring engagements. Determined to write something that recognised the contribution of black people and their heroes, he turned for inspiration to the Isley Brothers' 1970 single, 'Fight The Power'. He remembered it as being the first song he'd heard as a child that included cursing.

The director was suitably stunned when he took receipt of what many believe to be Public Enemy's finest five minutes. Lee had the good sense to highlight the song's shocking final verse, in which American icons Elvis Presley and John Wayne were summarily dismissed, before Chuck D added extra spite, slating sacred cow Presley as a 'straight-up racist'. Phew. *New York* magazine falsely believed the film and its subject matter would lead to full-scale rioting. Sound and vision had rarely gelled quite so perfectly. Lee returned the compliment by directing a video for the song, which re-enacted the 1963 civil rights march on Washington.

Chuck D fully expected to be taken to task for dissing the king of rock 'n' roll. What he didn't know was that 'minister of information' Professor Griff's anti-Semitic remarks (in an interview with David Mills) would overtake the group. Indeed, Spike Lee was forced to ring Chuck complaining of the 'heat' he was getting over Griff's remarks from studio executives.

Incidentally, Chuck's assertion that none of his heroes appear on stamps is wide of the mark. The first black person featured on a stamp was Booker T. Washington, in 1940. Martin Luther King's image has graced the American post as well as a long roll call of black musicians in the Black Heritage series.

Here's an oldie but goodie
Hit it!

Excuse me
What?
Can I have your attention? Mm-hmm.
There's just a few things that I've got to mention
(Uh-huh)
There's girlies out here that seem appealing
But they all come in your life and cold hurt
your feelings
I'm telling you, as Rick is my name
I wouldn't trust no girl unless she feels the same.

Treat 'em like a prostitute (Do what?)
Don't treat no girlie well until you're sure
of the scoop

It's your wife
You buy the tramp jewels and clothes
You get sentimental and bring home a rose
Give her everything 'cos you swear she's worth it
All your friends tell you, 'The bitch don't deserve it'
Love is blind, so there goes your wealth
Until one day, you see things for yourself
Came home from work early, Mr. Loverman
You had a card and some candy in your right hand
There's the mailman, he was short yet stout
He went inside your house and didn't come
back out
Bust it! Just a friendly stop, come on, is it?
The mailman comes and he pays your wife a visit?
The thought alone makes your temperature boil
You say to yourself, she might still be loyal
You open up your door and stand in a trance
You see the mailman's bag and the mailman's pants.

SLICK RICK
TREAT HER LIKE A PROSTITUTE
RELEASED 1988: INCLUDED ON: THE GREAT ADVENTURES OF SLICK RICK (1988)

Cos all they do is they hurt and trample
Listen up close, here comes my first example.

Now ya been with your girlfriend for quite a while
Plans for the future, she's having your child
Celebrate with friends drinking cans and quarts
Telling all your friends about your family thoughts
One friend was drunk so he starts to act wild
He tells the truth about the kid - it's not your child
Acting like a jerk and on his face was a smirk
He said, 'Your wife went berserk while you was
hard at work'
And she led him on and tried to please him
She didn't waste time, she didn't try to tease him.

Treat 'em like a prostitute (Do what?)
Don't treat no girlie well until you're sure
of the scoop
Cos all they do is they hurt and trample
Listen up close, here comes my second example.

Came home to party
At work had a hard day
Look around your house and you say,
'Where the hell are they?'
Run upstairs up to your bedroom
You look inside your room, you see
something brewin'
Cover your mouth because you almost choke…
You see the mailman's dick way up your
wife's throat.

Treat 'em like a prostitute (Mm-mm)
Don't treat no girlie well until you're sure
of the scoop
Cos all they do is they hurt and trample
Listen up close, here comes my last example.

Now your girl, she don't like to have sex a lot
And today she's ready and she's hot, hot, hot
As you open up the door she says, 'Get on the floor'
She wants to try things she's never tried before
She takes off your drawers and works you over
She calls you Twinkles and you call her Rover

SLICK RICK...

Next thing you know, the ho starts to ill
She says, 'I love you, Harold' and your name is Will
That's not the half, 'til you start to ride her
Take off your rubber and there's one more
inside her
It's not yours - who can it be?
I think it was a slick rapper, his name is
M.C. Ricky.

Treat 'em like a prostitute
Don't treat no girlie well, treat no girlie well
Treat no girlie well, until you're sure of the scoop.

Words & Music by Ricky Walters

No, it's not the erstwhile Ricky Walters' finest lyric (try 'Children's Story', also on his never-bettered *Great Adventures Of Slick Rick* album) but it is comfortably his most notorious. The eye-patched former Wimbledon native immersed himself in hip hop culture after moving to the Bronx with his Jamaican parents in 1985. He first worked with the Kangol Crew, made up of fellow students from La Guardia College of Music and Art, before teaming up with self-proclaimed 'human beatbox' Doug E. Fresh. The duo's 'La Di Da Di', released in 1985 as a double a-side with 'The Show', made both partners famous and highlighted Walters' (then known as Ricky D) way with a lascivious lyric.

The bawdy broadsides continued when he signed a solo deal with Def Jam. 1988's *The Great Adventures* shifted a million and a half copies on the back of hits such as 'Mona Lisa' and 'Hey Young World'. These were essays in street voyeurism enunciated in Rick's distinctive, sleepy English ex-pat tones (some American critics claimed he sounded like James Bond, but that exaggerates his vocal ethnicity). His sing-song style is credited as the inspiration behind fellow raconteurs of sleaze Snoop Dogg and Notorious B.I.G., two of many to acknowledge his pivotal influence. His label head Russell Simmons proclaimed him as the 'rapper's rapper' and Slick Rick seemed destined for super-stardom until he came off the rails in spectacular style (though in so doing he started another trend among rappers for collecting felonies as well as platinum discs). He shot estranged cousin Mark Plummer in 1990 believing his life to be in danger. One crazy car chase later the result was a three-to-ten stretch and a career strangled at birth. Though he issued a couple of albums on work release, with bail posted by Simmons, by the time he was back on the streets in the late 90s his efforts to make up time were doomed to failure. Hip hop, the most restless of art forms, had long since moved on and Rick's narratives now sounded dated.

But the *Great Adventures* remains one of the most influential rap albums of any era, and the rampant misogyny of 'Treat Her Like A Prostitute' has never gone out of fashion. Nowadays Rick's had time to reflect. 'I guess at the time I was going through my little problems with women, so this was from a guy's point of view,' he claimed in an interview with the *Hip Hop Connection*, while still incarcerated. 'You meet with a girl and after a while she sees someone cuter, she gets tired of you and she moves on. I guess I was a bit bitter about that time. That was a message to myself, or something.'

SLICK RICK

STETSASONIC...

As the sampling debate raged around hip hop – there were musicians still claiming that the practice was nothing more than artistic theft – Stetsasonic created this inspired riposte. The oft-quoted line 'Tell the truth, James Brown was old/Till Eric and Ra[kim] came out with 'I Got Soul'' succinctly undercut their detractors' arguments. As if to drive home the point, Stetsasonic constructed this song, the most enduring cut on one of hip hop's finest albums, on a double bass riff taken from Lonnie Liston Smith's 'Expansions'.

Brooklynites Stetsasonic introduced the world to two of hip hop's leading figures, Prince Paul and Daddy-O. Following a DJ battle in 1984 the quartet of Daddy-O, Delite, Fruitkwan, DBC and Wise invited Prince Paul, who'd been working as Biz Markie's DJ from the age of 13, into their ranks. They were marketed by Russell Simmons' Rush Management as 'the first hip hop band', and incorporated live instrumentation on stage as well as elaborate dance routines. Signed to Tommy Boy, their 1986 debut album *On Fire* was distinguished by the inclusion of 'A.F.R.I.C.A.', a song which heralded the first wave of Afrocentricity in hip hop.

But it was 1988's *In Full Gear* that saw them hit their stride. The radio hit 'Sally' was complemented by the hard-hitting 'Freedom Or Death', while 'Talkin' All That

Jazz' provided a touchstone moment that predicted the rise of jazz-rap. 'That really was an influential record on a coupla levels,' recalled label president Monica Lynch in the sleevenotes to *Tommy Boy's Greatest Beats* compilation. 'Not only did it have this really great jazz groove. Also, it addressed the whole sampling issue in a very upfront way... It was just that sampling at that time was a very grey area. It's still a controversial thing and there was that big argument over whether it was theft or art.'

As with most Stetsasonic tunes, the lyrics were penned by Daddy-O, with Prince Paul organising the beats. The impetus for the song came after the former was listening to a radio debate on sampling and became enraged by the direction the discussion was taking. As Prince Paul remembers: 'He was like, "But this whole sampling thing, if it wasn't for us a lot of these old cats that we been playing, especially in the parties and reviving, playing over it in the rap tunes, would really be by the wayside." James Brown – it's only because the rappers really brought him back out. Now he would have been looked on as some icon of funk music and an innovator, but nobody would be running his stuff as they do today or revere him as such a great guy if it wasn't for the MCs, and that goes with a lot of other artists as well.' He may just have a point, you know.

Lies, that's when you hide the truth
It's when you talk more jazz than proof
And when you lie and address something you
don't know
It's so wack that it's bound to show
When you lie about me and the band we get angry
We'll bite our pen, start writin' again
And the things we write are always true
Suckers, get a grip, now we talkin' 'bout you
Seems to me that you have a problem
So we can see what we can do to solve them
Think rap is a fad? You must be mad
Cos we're so bad we get respect you never had
Tell the truth, James Brown was old
Till Eric and Ra came out with 'I Got Soul'
Rap brings back old R&B
And if we would not, people could've forgot
We wanna make this perfectly clear
We're talented and strong and have no fear
Of those who choose to judge but lack pizazz.

Well here's how it started
Heard you on the radio talkin' 'bout rap
Sayin' all that crap about how we sample,
givin' examples
Think we'll let you get away with that?
You criticise our method of how we make records
You said it wasn't art, so now we're gonna
rip you apart.

Stop, check it out my man
This is the music of a hip-hop band
Jazz, well you can call it that
But this jazz retains a new format
Point, when you misjudged us
Speculated, created a fuss
You've made the same mistake politicians have.

STETSASONIC
TALKIN' ALL THAT JAZZ
RELEASED: 1988. INCLUDED ON: IN FULL GEAR (1988)

Talkin' all that jazz.

Talk, well I heard talk is cheap
But like beauty, talk is just skin deep
And when you lie and you talk a lot
People tell you to step off a lot
You see, you misunderstood
A sample is a tactic
A portion of my method, a tool
In fact it's only of importance when
I make it a priority
And what we sample's owned by the majority
But you are a minority, in terms of thought
Narrow minded and poorly taught
About hip-hop, playin' all the silly games
You erase my music, so no-one can use it
Step on us and we'll step on you
Can't have your cake and eat it too.

Talkin' all that jazz.

Talkin' all that jazz.

Now we're not tryin' to be a boss to you
We just wanna get across to you
That if you're talkin' jazz, the situation is a no-win
You might even get hurt, my friend
Stetsasonic, the hip-hop band
Like Sly and the Family Stone
We will stand up for the music we live and play
And for the song we sing today
For now, let us set the record straight
And later on we'll have a formal and informal
debate
But it's important you remember, though
What you reap is what you sow.

Talkin' all that jazz (x3).

Words & Music by Glenn Bolton
© Copyright 1988 T-Girl Music LLC, USA.
IQ Music Limited, Commercial House, 52 Perrymount Road,
Haywards Heath, West Sussex RH16 3DT.
All Rights Reserved. International Copyright Secured.

You got to have style, and learn to be original
And everybody's gonna wanna diss you
Like me, we stood up for the South Bronx
And every sucker MC had a response
You think we care? I know that they are on the tip
My posse from the Bronx is thick
And we're real live, we walk correctly
A lot of suckers would like to forget me
But they can't, cos like a champ
I have got a record of knocking out the frauds
in a second
On the mic, I believe that you should get loose
I haven't come to tell you I got juice
I just produce, create, innovate on a higher level
I'll be back, but for now just seckle!

Unidentified voice: So, you're a philosopher?
'Yes'
'I think very deeply [repeat]'

In about four seconds, the teacher will begin
to speak ...

Let's begin, what, where, why, or when
Will all be explained like instructions to a game
See I'm not insane, in fact, I'm kind of rational
When I be asking: 'Who is more dramatical?'
This one or that one, the white one or the
black one
Pick the punk, and I'll jump up to attack one

In about four seconds the teacher will
begin to speak ...

I'll play the nine and you play the target

BOOGIE DOWN PRODUCTIONS
MY PHILOSOPHY
RELEASED 1988: INCLUDED ON BY ALL MEANS NECESSARY (1988)

KRS-One is just the guy to lead a crew
Right up to your face and diss you
Everyone saw me on the last album cover
Holding a pistol, something far from a lover
Beside my brother, S-C-O-T-T
I just laughed, cos no one can defeat me

This is lecture number two, 'My Philosophy'
Number one was 'Poetry', you know it's me
This is my philosophy, many artists got to learn
I'm not flammable, I don't burn
So please stop burnin', and learn to earn respect
Cos that's just what KR collects
See, what do you expect when you rhyme like
a soft punk?
You walk down the street and get jumped

You all know my name so I guess I'll just start it
Or should I say, 'Start this'
I am an artist of new concepts at their hardest
Cos, yo! I'm a teacher and Scott is a scholar
It ain't about money cos we all make dollars
That's why I walk with my head up
When I hear wack rhymes I get fed up
Rap is like a set-up
A lot of games
A lot of suckers with colourful names
I'm so-and-so, I'm this, I'm that
Huh! but they all just wick-wick-wack
I'm not white or red or black I'm brown
From the Boogie Down Productions
Of course our music be thumpin'
Others say they're bad, but they're bugging
Let me tell you somethin' now about hip hop
About D-Nice, Melodie, and Scott La Rock
I'll get a pen, a pencil, a marker
Mainly what I write is for the average New Yorker
Some MCs be talkin' and talkin' tryin' to show

How black people are walkin'
But I don't walk this way to portray
Or reinforce stereotypes of today
Like all my brothers eat chicken and watermelon
Talk broken English and drug sellin'
See I'm telling, and teaching real facts
The way some act in rap is kind of wack
And it lacks creativity and intelligence
But they don't care cos the company is sellin' it
It's my philosophy, on the industry
Don't bother dissin' me
Or even wish that we'd soften, dilute, or
commercialise all the lyrics
Cos it's about time one of y'all hear it
And hear it first-hand from the intelligent
brown man
A vegetarian, no goat or ham
Or chicken or turkey or hamburger
Cos to me that's suicide - self-murder
Let us get back to what we call hip hop
And what it meant to DJ Scott La Rock ...

You're a philosopher?
'Yes, I think very deeply.'

In about four seconds the teacher will
begin to speak ...

How many MCs must get dissed
Before somebody says – 'Don't fuck with Kris!'
This is just one style, out of many
Like a piggy bank, this is one penny
My brother's name is Kenny - that's Kenny Parker
My other brother ICU is much darker

Boogie Down Productions is made up of teachers
The lecture is conducted from the mic into
the speaker
Who gets weaker? The king or the teacher?
It's not about a salary, it's all about reality
Teachers teach and do the world good
Kings just rule and most are never understood
If you were to rule or govern a certain industry
All inside this room right now would be in misery
No-one would get along nor sing a song
Cos everyone'd be singing for the king, am I wrong?

So yo, what's up? It's me again
Scott La Rock, KRS, BDP again
Many people had the nerve to think we would
end the trend
We're criminal minded, an album which is only ten
Funky, funky, funky, funky, funky hit records
No more than four minutes and some seconds
The competition checks and checks and keeps
checkin'
They buy the album, take it home, and start
sweating
Why? Well it's simple, to them it's kind of vital
To take KRS-One's title
To them I'm like an idol, some type of entity
In everybody's rhyme they wanna mention me?
Or rather mention us, me or Scott La Rock
But they can get bust get robbed, get dropped
I don't play around nor do I 'f' around
And you can tell by the bodies that are left around
When some clown jumps up to get beat down
Broken down to his very last compound
See how it sounds? A little unrational
A lot of MCs like to use the word DRAMATICAL!

Fresh for '88, you suckers ...

Words & Music by Lawrence Parker

BOOGIE DOWN
PRODUCTIONS...

Formed in the Bronx in 1984, BDP twinned then homeless rapper KRS-One (Lawrence Krisna Parker) with his DJ and social worker Scott La Rock (Scott Sterling). KRS-One (Knowledge Rules Supreme over almost every One) was immediately an impressive microphone stylist with a ferocious delivery – a dynamic serve-volleyer to the old school's backcourt players. But he wasn't just technically on-message - he also had a bright, questioning mind and the courage of his convictions. Indeed, throughout his career KRS-One has never ceased bigging himself up as the 'teacher' of hip hop values. If, by Henry Ford's definition, a bore is a fellow who opens his mouth and puts his feats in it, then KRS-One fits the bill, despite producing some blistering hip hop along the way.

BDP showed up on the radar after their feud with Marley Marl's Juice Crew kicked off the longest running and most celebrated 'diss war' in hip hop history. When Marley produced MC Shan's 'The Bridge' (a celebration of his Queensbridge neighbourhood), Boogie Down Productions slammed back with 'South Bronx'. Shan's follow-up told them to 'Kill That Noise'. Boogie Down Productions replied in the same register, without transparent levity, in the form of 'The Bridge Is Over'. These lyrical turf wars took place a few years before that sort of thing could land the rapper concerned in a mortuary. It also produced some glorious cutting edge music to match the cutting sarcasm.

BDP's *Criminal Minded*, released in 1987, is seen by many as a precursor to the gangsta rap movement, though its contents were more literate and quick-witted than much of the genre it helped inspire. Its stark urban warnings, articulated with panache by a rapper borrowing liberally from the Jamaican 'toasting' tradition, predicted real tragedy. By the end of the year La Rock had been shot dead while breaking up a fight. The following year KRS-1 signed Boogie Down Productions to Jive Records, adding his DJ brother Kenny Parker and D-Nice to the team and releasing *By All Means Necessary*, which opened with 'My Philosophy'. *Ghetto Music: The Blueprint Of Hip Hop* (1989), *Edutainment* (1990), *BDP Live Hardcore* (1991) and *Sex And Violence* (1992) followed. Thereafter KRS-One dropped the BDP moniker, releasing a series of albums (generally more thought-provoking than musically vital) and conducting lecture tours and writing articles. As well as inaugurating the Stop The Violence Movement and H.E.A.L. project, he has also collaborated with a bewildering array of artists, notably R.E.M. (on their 1991 single 'Radio Song'), reggae rhythm aces Sly and Robbie, Ziggy Marley, Billy Bragg and the Neville Brothers. He even scripted his own comic for Marvel.

'My Philosophy', its video directed by rap impresario Fab Five Freddy, provides a double scoop of KRS-One's lyrical preoccupations – ostentatious braggadocio backed by university-of-life wisdom. It's in the song's third verse that he really hits his flow, kicking back at black stereotypes, barking at the music biz for constraining the artistry and intelligence of hip hop while milking its audience of their dollars, and finally pleading with us to go back to the sort of hip hop that his fallen mentor, Scott La Rock, could relate to. Sometimes guilty of piety and sermonising, on 'My Philosophy' KRS-One is at his most heartfelt and compelling.

[MC Ren impersonating a court officer]
Right about now, N.W.A. court is in full effect
Judge Dre residing
In the case of N.W.A. vs. the Police Department
Prosecuting attourneys are: MC Ren, Ice Cube, and
Eazy-motherfuckin-E.

[Dr Dre impersonating the judge]
Order, order, order
Ice Cube, take the motherfuckin' stand
Do you swear to tell the truth, the whole truth
and nothin' but the truth
So help your black ass?

[Ice Cube impersonating a witness]
You god damn right!

[Dre]
Well, won't you tell everybody what the
fuck you gotta say?

Search a nigga down, and grabbin his nuts
And on the other hand, without a gun they
can't get none
But don't let it be a black and a white one
Cos they'll slam ya down to the street top
Black police showin' out for the white cop
Ice Cube will swarm
On any motherfucker in a blue uniform
Just cos I'm from, the CPT
Punk police are afraid of me!

Huh, a young nigga on the warpath
And when I'm finished
It's gonna be a bloodbath
Of cops, dying in L.A.
Yo Dre, I got somethin' to say.
('Fuck Tha Police')
Example of scene one -

N.W.A.

FUCK THA POLICE

RELEASED 1988: INCLUDED ON: STRAIGHT OUTTA COMPTON (1988)

[Ice Cube]
Fuck tha police comin' straight from
the underground
A young nigga got it bad cos I'm brown
And not the other colour
So police think
They have the authority to kill a minority
Fuck that shit
Cos I ain't the one
For a punk motherfucker with a badge and a gun
To be beatin' on
And thrown in jail
We can go toe to toe in the middle of a cell
Fucking with me cos I'm a teenager
With a little bit of gold and a pager
Searchin' my car, lookin' for the product
Thinkin' every nigga is selling narcotics
You'd rather see me in the pen
Than me and Lorenzo rollin in a Benz-o
Beat a police out of shape
And when I'm finished, bring the yellow tape
To tape off the scene of the slaughter
Still gettin swoll off bread and water
I don't know if they fags or what

[Police] Pull your goddamn ass over right now
[NWA] Aww shit, now what the fuck you
pullin' me over for?
[Police] Cos I feel like it! Just sit your ass on
the curb and shut the fuck up
[NWA] Man, fuck this shit
[Police] All right smartass, I'm takin' your
black ass to jail!

[Dre] MC Ren, will you please give your
testimony to the jury
about this fucked-up incident?

[MC Ren]
Fuck the police and Ren said it with authority
Because the niggas on the street is a majority
A gang is with whoever I'm steppin'
And the motherfuckin' weapon is kept in a stash box
For the so-called law
Wishin' Ren was a nigga that they never saw
Lights start flashin' behind me
But they're scared of a nigga
So they mace me to blind me
But that shit don't work, I just laugh

Because it gives 'em a hint not to step in my path
For police, I'm sayin', 'Fuck you, punk!'
Readin' my rights and shit, it's all junk
Pullin' out a silly club
So you stand with a fake-assed badge and a
gun in your hand
But take off the gun so you can see what's up
And we'll go at it punk, and I'ma fuck you up!
Make you think I'ma kick your ass
But drop your gat, and Ren's gonna blast
I'm sneaky as fuck when it comes to crime
But I'm gonna smoke 'em now and not next time
Smoke any motherfucker that sweats me
Or any asshole, that threatens me
I'm a sniper with a hell of a scope
Takin' out a cop or two, they can't cope with me
The motherfuckin' villain that's mad
With potential to get bad as fuck
So I'ma turn it around
Put in my clip, yo, and this is the sound
[GUNSHOTS]

Yeah, somethin' like that
But it all depends on the size of the gat
Takin' out a police would make my day
But a nigga like Ren don't give a fuck to say:

('Fuck Tha Police')

[Knocking on Door]

[NWA] Yeah, man, what you need?
[Police] Police, open now
[NWA] Aww shit
[Police] We have a warrant for Eazy-E's arrest
Get down and put your hands up where
I can see 'em
Move motherfucker, move now!
[NWA] What the fuck did I do, man
what did I do?
[Police] Just shut the fuck up and get your
motherfuckin' ass on the floor
(You heard the man, shut the fuck up!)
[NWA] But I didn't do shit
[Police] Man, just shut the fuck up!

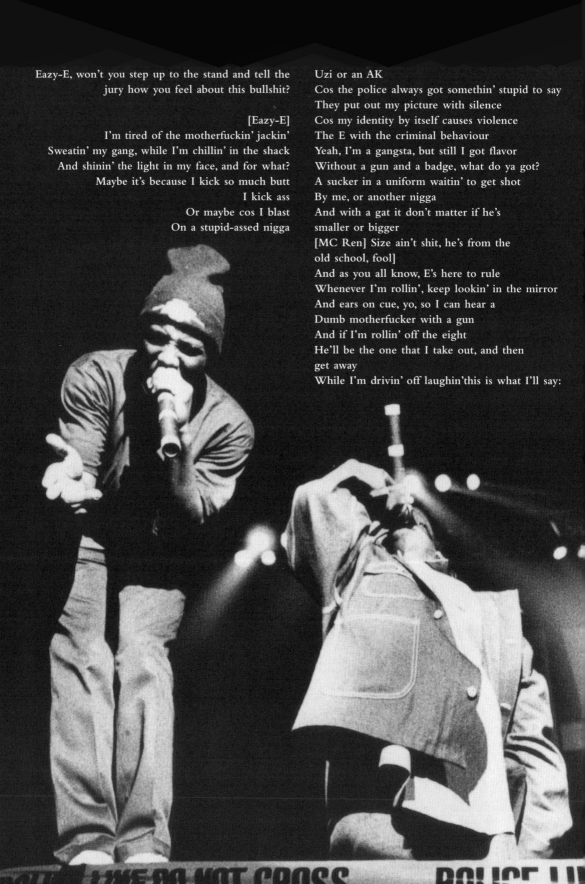

Eazy-E, won't you step up to the stand and tell the jury how you feel about this bullshit?

[Eazy-E]
I'm tired of the motherfuckin' jackin'
Sweatin' my gang, while I'm chillin' in the shack
And shinin' the light in my face, and for what?
Maybe it's because I kick so much butt
I kick ass
Or maybe cos I blast
On a stupid-assed nigga

Uzi or an AK
Cos the police always got somethin' stupid to say
They put out my picture with silence
Cos my identity by itself causes violence
The E with the criminal behaviour
Yeah, I'm a gangsta, but still I got flavor
Without a gun and a badge, what do ya got?
A sucker in a uniform waitin' to get shot
By me, or another nigga
And with a gat it don't matter if he's
smaller or bigger
[MC Ren] Size ain't shit, he's from the
old school, fool]
And as you all know, E's here to rule
Whenever I'm rollin', keep lookin' in the mirror
And ears on cue, yo, so I can hear a
Dumb motherfucker with a gun
And if I'm rollin' off the eight
He'll be the one that I take out, and then
get away
While I'm drivin' off laughin'this is what I'll say:

LINE DO NOT CROSS   POLICE LII

('Fuck Tha Police')

The verdict:

[Dre] The jury has found you guilty of bein'
a redneck, white bread, chickenshit motherfucker
[Police] But wait, that's a lie!
That's a goddamn lie!
[Dre] Get him out of here!
[Police] I want justice!
[Dre] Get him the fuck out my face!
[Police] I want justice!
[Dre] Out, right now
[Police] Fuck you, you black motherfuckers!

('Fuck The Police' x3)

DO NOT CROSS

N.W.A...

The clusterbomb detonation that was N.W.A.'s career is now part of rap's rich, bloody tapestry. A Los Angeles collective, N.W.A. essentially centred on the conflicting personalities of biz-savvy but mic-shy Eazy E, musical golden goose Dr Dre and devastating MC and lyricist Ice Cube. The group's debut album proper, *Straight Outta Compton* offered a barrage of obscenities and brutal narrative vignettes (and the hugely controversial appropriation of the word nigger, as advertised by their full title, Niggers With Attitude). Ugly yet compelling, this was hip hop reinvented as pure nihilism. It generated a national furore as moral guardians tumbled over themselves to express concern. The more they lambasted the 'moral vacuum' at the heart of N.W.A., the higher the spike on the group's sales graph. The album also drew a line in the sand for those representing the west coast. After N.W.A. the bohemia of New York rap seemed quaint in comparison to its mean-spirited, upstart west coast cousin.

Nothing was more explicit in setting out the group's agenda than 'Fuck Tha Police'. The song's targets, the police and the FBI, responded by claiming that the song 'encourages violence against and disrespect for the law enforcement officer'. Individual police departments, also warned about N.W.A, refused to provide concert security cover in several cities. At a show in Detroit the group members were warned that they'd be thrown in jail if they played 'FTP'. They wouldn't back down, played the song, and were arrested. 'Probably helped sell 500,000 more records,' reckons MC Ren. The song is actually a cogent mini-morality play, shuffling the group's pack of MCs. While Ren and Dre's impressions of authority figures are diverting, Ice Cube's interventions provide the dramatic backbone of the track.

'Fuck Tha Police' remains N.W.A.'s signature song. It is still cited by Def Jam's Russell Simmons as the finest rap record ever released (and it's most unlike him to advertise something that he has no vested interest in). In 2001, while contesting the efforts of Senator Joseph Liberman to penalise 'record labels who market obscene material to young people', Simmons likened the song to those written in the protest tradition of Bob Dylan, arguing that it highlighted racial profiling by American police forces years before that term came into vogue.

GANG STARR...

Gang Starr, a pairing of Guru (Keith Elam) and
DJ Premier (Chris Martin), have greatly expanded
hip hop's musical frontiers over the last decade
and a half. Though they have rarely been afforded
the newsprint more attention-seeking peers have
enjoyed, it doesn't seem to bother them too much.
A teaming of considerable grey matter (they boast
management and computer science degrees
between them) they united after Guru discovered
one of Premier's demo tapes in 1988. Putting aside
a variety of non-firing earlier projects, they initially
collaborated by posting tapes while each was
based in different cities.

Debut single 'Manifest' featured samples from
Dizzy Gillespie's 'A Night In Tunisia' alongside the
customary James Brown steals. Together with
'Jazz Music', 'Manifest' sought to break down the
walls between hip hop and jazz, reconciling them
as tributaries springing from the same artistic
gene pool. There's an obvious genre-blurring
precursor here in Stetsasonic's 'Talkin' All That
Jazz', but Gang Starr (and Guru's later
collaborations with live jazz musicians as part of
the Jazzmatazz project) cemented the notion of
jazz-rap as a viable musical genre.

The lyrics on 'Jazz Music' provided a roll call of
jazz inspirations, invoked by nickname, but there
was also an acknowledgement of the indignities of
slavery that forged black music in the first place.
When Spike Lee invited the duo to contribute to
his *Mo' Better Blues* soundtrack, Guru and
Premier went back to the drawing board,
redrafting a longer version of the lyric and inviting
Branford Marsalis to jointly remodel the song
as 'Jazz Thing', a triumph of musicality as well
as a mission statement.

The magic of Gang Starr has always revolved
around the easy fit between Guru's laconic
narration and knowing lyrics and Premier's often
inspired melodic scheming.

Gang Starr have emerged as one of the limited
number of hip hop acts to enjoy a sustained career
without losing focus or facing slipping sales.
However, the definitive *Full Clip – A Decade Of
Gang Starr* (1999), which includes such touchstone
tracks as 'Credit Is Due', 'Just To Get A Rep' and
'You Know My Steez' should be your starting point
(it also includes a video version of 'Jazz Thing').

It's jazz music... jazz music.

Yo, the music that Pops and other cats made,
it stayed
Cos people love when they played
To the north, it took a riverboat shuffle
To the big cities, with lots of hustle and bustle
To Chicago, and to the Apple too
This was a scene that our forefathers knew
Go get your crew
I know they'll get into the jazz music...
jazz music.

The music started in the hearts and drums,
from another land
Played for everyone, by sons of the motherland
Sending out a message of peace, to everybody
And came across the oceans in chains and shame
Easing the pain, and it was without name
Until some men in New Orleans on
Rampart Street
Put out the sounds, and then they gave it a beat
I'm talkin' 'bout Jelly Roll, King, and Satch
I'm talkin' 'bout the music that had no match
Yes the music, and it was born down there
We're gonna use it, so make the horn sound clear.

The music called jazz had the razzamatazz
It had the flavor, and a lot of pizazz
The big band beat was very neat and unique
The swing was king, it made you tap your feet
There was Benny and Duke and of course the

GANG STARR
JAZZ MUSIC
RELEASED 1989: INCLUDED ON NO MORE MR NICE GUY (1989)

GANG STARR

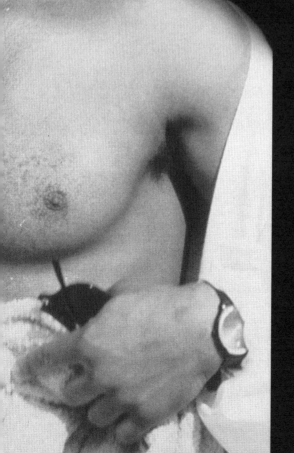

Count Basie
The melody was smooth and yes, very tasty
There was Hap, The Prez, and Lady Day
And Dizzy Bird and Miles
They were all playin'
They brought it to the people of the foreign lands
Back across the oceans and the desert sands
Where it echoes in the distant sounds of drums
And it rises with the sun on days begun
This is the music that we give tribute to
They gave it to us, that's why we give it to you.

The jazz music... the jazz music
The jazz music...

Words & Music by Chris Martin, Keith Elam,
Elliot Horne & Schlomo Sonnenfeld
© Copyright 1989 Frozen Soap Songs/Raybird Music/
Irving Music Incorporated, USA.
Rondor Music (London) Limited, 10A Parsons Green,
London SW6 4TW.
All Rights Reserved. International Copyright Secured.

[Dove]
Proud, I'm proud of what I am
Poems I speak are Plug Two type
Please oh please let Plug Two be himself
Not what you read or write
Write is wrong when hype is written on the Soul
De La that is
Style is surely our own thing
Not the false disguise of show-biz
De La Soul is from the soul
And in fact I can't deny
Strictly from the Dan called Stuckie
And from me myself and I.

It's just me myself and I (x3).

[Posdnuos]
Glory Glory Hallelu
Glory for Plugs One and Two
But that glory's been denied

DE LA SOUL
ME, MYSELF AND I
RELEASED: 1989. INCLUDED ON: 3 FEET HIGH AND RISING (1989)

[Dove]
Mirror mirror on the wall
Tell me mirror what is wrong?
Can it be my De La clothes
Or is it just my De La song?
What I do ain't make believe
People say I sit and try
But when it comes to being De La
It's just me myself and I.

It's just me myself and I (x3).

[Posdnuos]
Now you tease my Plug One style
And my Plug One spectacles
You say Plug One and Two are hippies
No we're not, that's pure Plug Bull
Always pushin' that we formed an image
There's no need to lie
When it comes to being Plug One

It's just me myself and I.

It's just me myself and I (x3).

By concensing dookie-eyes
People think they diss my person
By stating I'm darkly packed
I know this so I point at Q-Tip
And he states 'Black is Black'.

Mirror mirror on the wall
Shovel chestnuts in my path
Just keep all nuts twistin' up
So I don't get an aftermath
But if I do I'll calmly punch them in the
4th day of July
Cos they tried to mess with third degree
That's me myself and I.

It's just me myself and I (x3) .

*Words & Music by David Jolicoeur, Paul Huston, Vincent Mason,
Kelvin Mercer, George Clinton, Phil Wynn & Edwin Birdsong*
© *Copyright 1988 Bridgeport Music Incorporated (50%)/
T-Girl Music LLC/Edwin Birdsong Music Publishing, USA.
IQ Music Limited (25%)/Notting Hill Music (UK) Limited (25%).
All Rights Reserved. International Copyright Secured.*

DE LA SOUL...

De La Soul announced themselves in 1989 with the delicious musicality of *3 Feet High And Rising*. Bouncing super-smart rhymes off a bewildering array of samples, combining musical idioms and sprinkling the results with natural, unforced humour, De La Soul made the suburbs of Amityville, Long Island, sound like rap's bohemian capital. Hip hop hippies who invoked the term *daisy age* rap then quickly disowned it, the vibrant trio of Posdnuos (Kelvin Mercer), Trugoy the Dove (David Jolicoeur) and Pasemaster Mase (Vincent Mason) took the primary colours of rap's easel and blended irreverent new pigments.

The musical policy was larceny on an epic scale, snatching cast-off psychedelic rock riffs, bubblegum pop phrases and reggae riddims as well as mining the traditional hip hop wellsprings of funk and soul. As the album's cover informed you, De La Soul were painting with big wax crayons and crazy colours, while the contents were themed around a quiz show, helping to popularise the rap album skit. A landmark album by any measure, it brought Tommy Boy Records its first gold sales ratification.

The group were signed to Tommy Boy on the advice of Prince Paul of Stetsasonic after he heard a demo of 'Plug Tunin', an early example of their creative approach to sampling – using 'found sound' to create new textures rather than just as convenient hooks on which to hang rhymes. Hit singles included 'The Magic Number' but also the agenda-setting individualism of 'Me Myself And I'. It seemed to complement Public Enemy's blistering rhetoric, enlarging hip hop's appeal without compromising its ethics. 'Me Myself And I' was hardly the first rap record to sample George Clinton (in this case 'Not Just Knee Deep'), but De La Soul also shared his taste for the surreal, rather than the 'keep it real' mantra of modern rappers to come.

Monica Lynch of Tommy Boy distinguishes the group from the prevailing mass of 'brag-rappers': 'At that time rap was starting to fall into clichés or creating styles that were not inclusive of the whole rap audience. They were the antidote to the prevailing macho, leather and chains aesthetic.' Over a decade on *3 Feet High And Rising* still serves as a reminder of the endless possibilities of hip hop.

DE LA SOUL

TONE LOC...

That old frontier epithet – that the pioneers get the arrows, the settlers get the land – is certainly true of hip hop. Of the pop-rappers who plundered chart success in the 80s and 90s, it's easy to draw a line in the sand between figures of fun (Vanilla Ice and MC Hammer) and the sassily credible Salt N'Pepa and Tone Loc. The latter just happened to catch the nation's mood perfectly and didn't overstay his welcome.

While everyone else was following the adventures of N.W.A., Anthony Terrell Smith offered us sunshine and romance – delivered by a gravel-voiced heavyweight who was every bit as capable of standing his ground as the Ice Cubes and T's of this world. He was running with LA gangs when Delicious Vinyl's owners Matt Dike and Mike Ross asked him to rap over a track that used a sample of Van Halen's 'Jamie's Cryin'. Ross remembers: 'When I just heard him speak it was like – you're the man. 'Cos his voice was just... he was just so smooth, his voice was so sexy and cool. If we get him on the right tracks this could blow up.'

Ross's faith was rewarded when this libidinous eulogy to girl chasing did just that. It reached number two in the American charts and became the biggest selling single of the decade behind charity effort 'We Are The World'. This was due in no small part to rotation play on MTV, and a video that was the rap equivalent of Robert Palmer's 'Addicted To Love'.

Both 'Wild Thing' and the similarly successful 'Funky Cold Medina' were co-written by Tone's Delicious Vinyl labelmate, Young MC, who reckons his contribution took him less than half an hour. 'I came up with "Wild Thing" initially,' says Tone. 'It was a little bit dirty, a little bit wild... "Wild Thing" was never my style of rap song that I would write. But, you know, the song became big and what the heck – I'm like the Chuck Berry of rap.'

Tone subsequently become the first African American rapper to top the Billboard pop album chart. He also introduced the wider world to production whizz kids the Dust Brothers (Dike and radio DJs John King and John Simpson), whose 'symphonic compression of samples' would later be heard to stunning effect on the Beastie Boys' *Paul's Boutique*. Thereafter Tone's career faltered as he found it impossible to escape from the shadow of his 'Wild Thing' persona, though he enjoyed some success after switching to acting.

Let's do it!

Workin' all week nine to five for my money
So when the weekend comes I go get live
with the honey
Rollin' down the street I saw this girl and
she was pumpin'
I winked my eye she got into the ride went
to a club – was jumpin'
Introduce myself as Loc she said 'You're a liar'
I said 'I got it goin' on baby doll and I'm on fire'
Took her to the hotel she said 'You're the king'
I said 'Be my queen if you know what I mean
And let us do the wild thing!'.

Wild thing
Wild thing.

Shoppin' at the mall looking for some gear to buy
I saw this girl she cold-rocked my world and
I had to adjust my fly

Took her to the limousine still parked outside
I tipped the chauffeur when it was over and
I gave her my own ride
Couldn't get her off my jack she was like static cling
But that's what happens when body start slappin'
from doin' the wild thing.

Wild thing
She wanna do the wild thing
Please baby, baby please.

Wild thing.

Doin' a little show at the local discotheque
This fine young chick was on my jack so
I say what the heck
She want to come on stage and do her little dance
So I said chill for now but maybe later
you'll get your chance

TONE ·LOC
WILD THING
RELEASED: 1988. INCLUDED ON: LOC'ED AFTER DARK (1989)

She looked at me and smiled and said
'You have plans for the night?'
I said 'Hopefully if things go well I'll be
with you tonight'
So we journeyed to her house one thing
led to another
A key in the door, I cold-hit the floor
looked up and it was her mother
I didn't know what to say I was hanging by a string
She said 'Hey, you two, I was once like you
And I liked to do the wild thing'.

Wild thing
She loved to do the wild thing
Wild thing
Please baby, baby please.

Posse in effect hangin' out is always hype
And when me and the crew leave the shindig
I want a girl who's just my type
Saw this luscious little frame I ain't
lyin' fellas, she was fine
The sweet young miss go gave me a kiss
and I knew that she was mine

So when the show was finished I took
her around the way
And what do you know she was good to
go without a word to say
We was all alone and she said 'Tone, let me
tell you one thing
I need $50 to make you holler I get paid to
do the wild thing'.

Say what?
Yo, love, you must be kidding
You're walkin', babe
Just break out of here
Hasta la vista baby!

Wild thing.

(Begins with channel-surfing samples)

On a brighter note...
Commercial break...
The government has now banned the
carrying of spears...
Stop about every 1,000 miles ain't asking
too much, is it?
You may wish to stay on and listen...
It was a place where everything was legal...
(CHOIR)
I met this woman...
If you're looking for emotional satisfaction,
My advice to you is: seek professional help...

Thank you for joining us live on the air

And apartheid is a new headache remedy.

Absorbed in its world it's so hard to find us
It shapes our minds the most
Maybe the mother of our nation should remind us
That we're sitting too close to –

Television, the drug of the nation
Breeding ignorance and feeding radiation (x2)

TV is the stomping ground for political candidates
Where bears in the woods are chased by
Grecian Formula'd bald eagles
TV is mechanized politics' remote control
over the masses
Co-sponsored by environmentally safe gases
Watch for the PBS special
It's the perpetuation of the two-party system
Where image takes precedence over wisdom

DISPOSABLE HEROES OF HIPHOPRISY

TELEVISION, THE DRUG OF THE NATION

RELEASED 1988 (IN ITS ORIGINAL FORM BY THE BEATNIGS)
INCLUDED ON: HYPOCRISY IS THE GREATEST LUXURY (1992)

My pleasure.

One nation under God
Has turned into one nation under the influence
of one drug –

Television, the drug of the nation
Breeding ignorance and feeding radiation (x2)

TV - it satellite links our United States
of Unconsciousness
Apathetic, therapeutic and extremely addictive
The methadone metronome pumping out
150 channels 24 hours a day
You can flip through all of them and still
there's nothing worth watching
TV is the reason why less than ten per cent
of our nation reads books daily
Why most people think Central America
means Kansas
Socialism means unamerican

Where soundbite politics are served to the
fast food culture
Where straight teeth in your mouth are
more important
Than the words that come out of it
Race-baiting is the way to get selected
Willie Horton or will he not get elected on –

Television, the drug of the nation
Breeding ignorance and feeding radiation (x2)

MORE TV SAMPLES

TV – is it the reflector or the director?
Does it imitate us or do we imitate it?
Because a child watches 1,500 murders
before he's twelve years old

And we wonder why we've created
a Jason generation
That learns to laugh rather than to abhor the horror.

TV – is the place where armchair generals
and quarterbacks
Can experience first hand the excitement
. of video warfare
As the theme song is sung in the background
Sugar sweet sitcoms that leave us with a
bad actor taste
While pop stars metamorphosize into soda pop stars.

You saw the video
You heard the soundtrack
Well, now go buy the soft drink
Well, the only cola that I support would be a union

C.O.L.A.(Cost Of Living Allowance) on –

Television, the drug of the nation
Breeding ignorance and feeding radiation (x2)

MORE TV SAMPLES

Back again, 'New and improved'
We return to our irregularly programmed schedule
Hidden cleverly between heavy-breasted beer
and car commercials
CNN-ESPN-ABC-TNT: but mostly B.S.
Where oxymoronic language like 'virtually spotless',
'Fresh frozen', 'light yet filling'
And 'military intelligence' have become standard
TV is the place where phrases are redefined
like 'recession' to 'necessary downturn'
'Crude oil' on a beach to 'mousse'
'Civilian death' to 'collateral damages'
And being killed by your own army is now
called 'friendly fire'.

TV is the place where the pursuit of happiness
has become the pursuit of trivia
Where toothpaste and cars have become sex objects
Where imagination is sucked out of children
by a cathode ray nipple
TV is the only wet nurse that would
create a cripple.

Television, the drug of the nation
Breeding ignorance and feeding radiation (x4)

Words & Music by Michael Franti & Mark Pistel

DISPOSABLE HEROES OF HIPHOPRISY

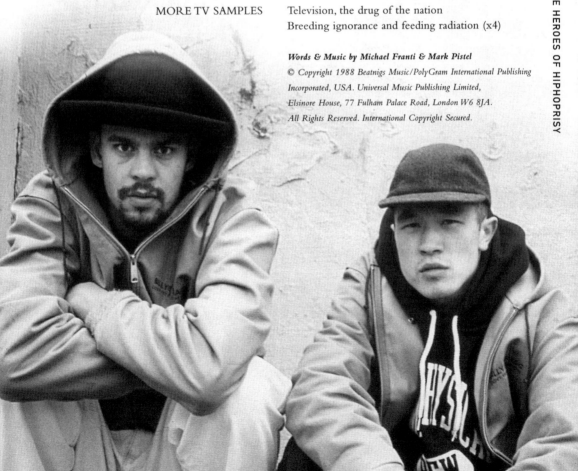

DISPOSABLE HEROES OF HIPHOPRISY...

The Disposable Heroes are an act readily dismissed as rap apologists by many, and often cited alongside the likes of Arrested Development and PM Dawn as funk-free PC polemicists who want to sanitise hip hop. And they have a point – Michael Franti's politically-nuanced lyrics owe much to the narrative lineage of the beat poets and provide a break from existing hip hop traditions and reference points. But that's not necessarily a bad thing. The post-punk, industrial/metallic clangfest that musical partner Rono Tse whipped up may not have had the party jumping, but its genre-bending was authentically inventive in the spirit, if not the image of old school legend Afrika Bambaataa. Together they produced one riveting album and Franti a batch of lyrics that were supremely eloquent, if a little austere and didactic for some tastes.

With themes couched in the civil rights vernacular of the Last Poets and Gil Scott-Heron, *Hypocrisy Is The Greatest Luxury* adroitly attacked rap's preoccupations with materialism while providing detailed critiques of American foreign policy, the military-industrial complex, East-West relations, homophobia, violence and Uncle Tom-ism (specifically 'Famous And Dandy (Like Amos And Andy)'s allusions to the artistic cannibalism of rap's modern minstrels). The free jazz to post-industrial backdrop helped Franti thump home the tracts, none of which was more compelling than his ode to the brain-shrivelling cultural microwave that is modern American television.

The song's genesis can be traced back to the duo's former incarnation as part of San Francisco's anarchic coalition, the Beatnigs, who recorded one excellent album for Jello Biafra's Alternative Tentacles label (they later cut a version of 'California Uber Alles' in tribute to Biafra's Dead Kennedys – a testament to their punk influences). Re-recorded to promote *...Luxury*, 'Television' brought them glowing reviews in broadsheet newspapers, who saw in Franti someone as articulate as Public Enemy's Chuck D without the baggage. In the process the line 'Imagination is sucked out of children by a cathode ray nipple/

TV is the only wet nurse that would create a cripple' briefly became the most quoted rap couplet since Chuck's gang were telling us what they really thought of Elvis. The sleevenotes, however, had to include an acknowledgement that Grecian Formula 'is a registered trademark of Combe Inc.'. Such is the world we live in.

But that was it for the aptly titled Disposable Heroes. Hip hop heads weren't 'feelin" it', apparently. Franti, sensitive to critical barbs from within the rap community, dissolved the group and moved on to form Spearhead, a more R&B-orientated vehicle that has gone some way to appeasing his detractors (he still gives great lyric, however).

2 LIVE CREW...

2 Live Crew are the dream ticket for sceptics of rap music, a group satisfying every criticism on every conceivable level. Yet Luther 'Luke Skyywalker' Campbell, Mark Ross (a.k.a. Brother Marquis), Christopher WongWon (a.k.a. Fresh Kid Ice) and David Hobbs (a.k.a. Mr Mixx) are an integral part of any history of rap music due to the sandstorm that blew up around their 'obscene' lyrics in 1989.

Had that not been the case nobody would ever have heard of the group outside of Florida, where they helped popularise Miami Bass music. This hip hop-funk variant was characterised by voluminous jeep and 4x4 stereo systems, whose rumbling bass registered unquantifiable damage on the foundations of Florida's homesteads. Above these subsonic vibrations was a complex lyrical dialectic concerning the amplitude of a lady's nether regions, repeated *ad nauseum*. 2 Live Crew's 'Throw The D' in 1986 was a benchmark release in this torrid sub-genre, but it was with 1989's *As Nasty As They Wanna Be* that they really caught fire, thanks principally to 'Me So Horny'. Built around a sample of a Vietnamese prostitute

taken from *Full Metal Jacket*, and featuring musical lifts from Mass Productions' 'Firecracker', 'Me So Horny' saw its creators engulfed in a bizarre censorship odyssey.

In June 1990 a federal judge in Florida deemed *As Nasty As They Wanna Be* 'obscene'. Freedom of speech veterans including Bruce Springsteen (and Donny Osmond) lined up in the band's defence – who then issued a 'clean' version that absolutely no-one was interested in. The fact that the album contained 87 separate references to oral sex did not pass without mention, as right-wing lawyer Jack Thompson got his teeth stuck into the case. But the attitude of anyone with any sense was, if you ignore these people, they will eventually go away. And they did, to all intents and purposes, though they later adapted their lyrics to accommodate rising concerns about safe sex. 2 Live Crew certainly pushed the boundaries of libertarianism – in their case, the freedom to say whatever you like, no matter how stoopid – but they were an important first amendment test case. And no band who lists *their entire fan club* on the CD cover of their album, as they did on *As Nasty As They Wanna Be*, can be totally beyond redemption. Can they?

[sample from Full Metal Jacket]

What'll we get for ten dollars?
Every 'ting you want
Everything?
Every'ting
Ooh! Don't do that, baby! Ahh!
Hold on this!
Oh, sock it to me! Aaahh!
Ooohh!

[sample from Full Metal Jacket]

Ahh! Me so horny!
Me love you long time!

[Brother Marquis]
Sittin' at home with my dick on hard
So I got the black book for a freak to call
Picked up the telephone, then dialled the
seven digits

Ahh! Me so horny!
Me love you long time!

[Brother Marquis]
You can say I'm desperate, even call me perverted
But you say I'm a dog when I leave you
fucked and deserted
I'll play with your heart just like it's a game
I'll be blowing your mind while you're
blowing my brains
I'm just like that man they call Georgie Puddin' Pie
I fuck all the girls and I make 'em cry
I'm like a dog in heat, a freak without warning
I have an appetite for sex, cos me so horny.

Ahh! Me so horny!
Me love you long time!

Ahh! Hold on this! Oh, sock it to me!

2 LIVE CREW
ME SO HORNY
RELEASED 1989: INCLUDED ON AS NASTY AS THEY WANNA BE (1989)

Said, 'Yo, this Marquis, baby! Are you down with it?'
I arrived at her house, knocked on the door
Not having no idea of what the night had in store
I'm like a dog in heat, a freak without warning
I have an appetite for sex, cos me so horny.

Ahh! Me so horny!
Me love you long time!

[Fresh Kid Ice]
Girls always ask me why I fuck so much
I say 'What's wrong, baby doll, with a quick nut?'
Cos you're the one, and you shouldn't be mad
I won't tell your mama if you don't tell your dad
I know he'll be disgusted when he sees your
pussy busted
Won't your mama be so mad if she knew
I got that ass?
I'm a freak in heat, a dog without warning
My appetite is sex, cos me so horny.

Ahh! Me so horny!
Me love you long time!

[Fresh Kid Ice]
It's true, you were a virgin until you met me
I was the first to make you hot and wetty-wetty
You tell your parents that we're goin' out
Never to the movies, just straight to my house
You said it yourself, you like it like I do
Put your lips on my dick, and suck my asshole too
I'm a freak in heat, a dog without warning
My appetite is sex, cos me so horny.

Ahh! Me so horny!
Me love you long time!

Fuckie suckie. Me fuckie suckie.

Words & Music by Luther Campbell, David Hobbs, Mark Ross,
Ricardo Williams & Christopher Wongwon
© Copyright 1989 Pac-Jam Publishing/Two Pepper Music, USA.
Universal/MCA Music Limited, Elsinore House,
77 Fulham Palace Road, London W6 8JA.

I heard payback's a motherfucking nigga
That's why I'm sick of getting treated like a
goddamn stepchild
Fuck a punk cos I ain't him
You gotta deal with the nine-double-M
The damn scum that you all hate
Just think if niggas decide to retaliate
They try to keep me from running up
I never tell you to get down, it's all about
coming up
So what they do go and ban the AK?
My shit wasn't registered any fucking way
So you better duck away, run and hide out
When I'm rolling real slow and the lights out
Cos I'm about to fuck up the program
Shooting out the window of a drop-top Brougham
When I'm shooting let's see who drop
The police, the media and suckers that went pop
And motherfuckers that say they too black
Put 'em overseas they be begging to come back
They say keep 'em on gangs and drugs

Any Tom Dick and Hank or get the ass fake
It ain't about how right or wrong you live
But how long you live
I ain't with the bullshit
I meet cold bitches no hoes
Don't wanna sleep so I keep popping – no doze
And tell the young people what they gotta know
Cos I hate when niggas gotta live low
And if you're locked up I dedicate my style in
From San Quentin to Rykers Island
We got 'em afraid of the funky shit
I like to clown so pump up the sound in the jeep
Make the old ladies say 'Oh my God, wait –
It's the nigga ya love to hate'

Yeah, come on fool
It's the nigga you love to hate
Yeah, run up punk
It's the nigga you love to hate
('Bitch! I ain't nobody's bitch!')

ICE CUBE

THE NIGGA YA LOVE TO HATE

RELEASED: 1990. INCLUDED ON: AMERIKKKA'S MOST WANTED (1990)

You wanna sweep a nigga like me up under the rug.

Kicking shit called street knowledge
Why more niggas in the pen than in college?
Now cos of that line I might be your cellmate
That's from the nigga ya love to hate.

Yeah, ha-ha, it's the nigga you love to hate
Baby, your mother warned you about me
It's the nigga you love to hate
What you got to say for yourself?
You do like how I'm living? Well, fuck you.

Once again it's on, the motherfucking psycho
Ice Cube the bitch killa cap peeler
Yo, runnin' through the line like Bo
It's no pot to piss in
I put my fist in
Now who do ya love to hate?
Cos I talk shit and down the eight-ball
Cos I don't fake you're begging I fall off
The crossover might as well cut them balls off
And get your ass ready for the lynching
The mob is droppin' common sense
And we'll gank in the pen will shank

A bitch is a...
Soul Train done lost they soul
Just call it train, cos the bitches look like hoes
I see a lotta others, damn
It almost look like the Bandstand
You ask me did I like Arsenio?
About as much as the bicentennial
I don't give a fuck about dissing these fools
Cos they all scared of the Ice Cube
And what I say what I portray an' all that
And ain't even seen the gat
I don't wanna see no dancing
I'm sick of that shit
Listen to the hit
Cos yo if I look and see another brother
On the video tryin' to out-dance each other
I'm a tell T-Bone to pass the bottle
And don't give me that shit about role model
It ain't wise to chastise and preach
Just open the eyes of each
Cos laws are made to be broken up
What niggas need to do is start loc-ing up
And build, mould and fold theyself into shape.

Of the nigga ya love to hate

ICE CUBE...

O'Shea Jackson played a leading role in the genesis of gangsta rap as the most accomplished MC with Compton pioneers N.W.A., before quitting over management disputes.

While his former compatriots persevered without him, throwing occasional lyrical jibes his way, Cube readied for his solo bow. On the controversial but visceral *AmeriKKKa's Most Wanted*, he confirmed that he was always the real talent in the band (Dr Dre's production skills would only earn recognition after he embarked on his own solo career). It saw him introduce his extended family Da Lench Mob (headed by childhood friend and Dre's cousin, Sir Jinx). More importantly he dispensed with regional rivalries and headed east to cut the record with Public Enemy's Bomb Squad (Hank and Bill Shocklee and Chuck D with Eric 'Vietnam' Sadler). Their firestorm sonics segued beautifully with Cube's scalding rhymes in month-long sessions in New York. Though there were concessions to Cube and Jinx's love of classic funk, they still couldn't resist throwing a few police sirens into the mix.

Even compared to N.W.A. the results were indignant, consumed with resentment and anger. The album saw Cube lashing out like a punch-drunk boxer. Sometimes the blows were low (particularly in the case of 'You Can't Fade Me' as he contemplates kicking 'the bitch in the tummy' after discovering an unwanted pregnancy) But when Cube did hit bullseye, as on the scathing 'The Nigga Ya Love To Hate', it was compulsive stuff.

Following the grisly execution sketch 'Better Off Dead', 'Nigga' starts the album and sets its agenda. The song splices N.W.A.'s nihilism with Public Enemy's revolutionary tracts, glocks *and* spiel, if you like. While 'Nigga' throws down the kind of imposing threats that characterise Ice Cube as an MC (he is unsurpassed in all of hip hop-dom for his ability to cuss) there's also exasperation at the black man's condition. 'Why more niggas in the pen than in college?' he asks, before blazing away again. This is unapologetic retaliatory music that throws bile at the mainstream of black culture (*Soul Train*, *Arsenio Hall*). And the lyrics are tellingly dismissive about those programmes' emphasis on positivity. 'It ain't about how right or wrong you live,' he notes. 'But how long you live.'

Words & Music by O'Shea Jackson, Eric Sadler, Buddy Hank, David Spradley, Steve Arrington, Charles Carter, Gary Shider, Roger Parker & George Clinton

ICE CUBE

CYPRESS HILL...

More than any other contemporary hip hop entity, multi-racial Los Angeles trio Cypress Hill are responsible for ennobling spliff culture as the dominant lyrical motif of rap in the 90s. But theirs was no doped-up peace 'n' love vibe. Unlike De La Soul's bright-eyed, bushy-tailed take on hippy culture, Cypress Hill's vision was intensely bleak, sinister and menacing.

Comprising Italian DJ Muggs and Latino MCs B-Real and Sen Dog, the trio took their name from their locale in Southgate, Los Angeles, which was within drive-by distance of N.W.A.'s Compton. Their debut album eventually achieved platinum sales after this song and accompanying singles 'Latin Lingo' and 'Hand On The Pump' primed an audience that was never strictly 'ghetto'. Instead their knotty, tough-sinewed musicality and love of the macabre saw them embraced by rock audiences as no other rap crew outside of Run-D.M.C. and Public Enemy had been before. 'How I Could Just Kill A Man', in particular, heralded their crossover success after it featured at the climax of Ernest Dickerson's hit film *Juice*.

'How I Could Just Kill A Man' sets out Cypress Hill's murky agenda with its idle, carefree boasts about plugging anyone who trifles with their crew. B-Real's oddly compelling whine and Muggs's bleary, groping-mist production built a musical tension that established a new rap paradigm – hardcore fans would no longer accept beats that were anything less than head-noddingly hypnotic. The recurring 'What does it all mean?' sample, incidentally, is lifted from Double D and Steinski's sample-and-scratch epic 'Payoff Mix'.

For most critics Cypress Hill never revisited the highs of their debut – though they continued to talk *about* highs incessantly. While Muggs was venerated as the hottest producer on the west coast outside of Dr Dre, the band's subsequent output observed the law of diminishing returns, and the constant talk of gats and blunts paled. Second album *Black Sunday*'s 'When The Shit Goes Down' offered a back-reference to the song that first established them in the line 'Hot damn, I didn't want to kill a man'. Other signs of contrition were conspicuous by their absence, however.

[Intro]
It's another one of them ol' funky
Cypress Hill things
You know what I'm sayin'?
And it goes like this –

[Be-Real]
Hey don't miss out on what your passin'
You're missin' the hoota of the funky
Buddha Eluder
Or the fucked up styles to get wicked
So come on as Cypress starts to kick it
Cos we're like the outlaw stridin'
Suckers are hiding
Jump behind the bush when they see me driving by
Hangin' out my window
With my magnum takin' out some puto's
Acting kinda loco
I'm just another local kid from the street getting
paid for my vocals.

How I could just kill a man!
One-time tried to come in my home,
take my chrome
I said 'Yo, it's on. Take cover son, or you're ass-out.
How you like my chrome?'
Then I watched the rookie pass out
Didn't have to blast him, but I did anyway
[Laughter]
That young punk had to pay
So I just killed a man!

[Chorus]

[Be-Real]
It's gonna be a long time before I finish one
of the many missions
That I have to establish
To light my spliff, ignite ya with these sights
And if you ain't down: bullshit!
Say some punk try to get you for your auto
Would you call the one-time, play the role model?

CYPRESS HILL
HOW I COULD JUST KILL A MAN
RELEASED: 1991. INCLUDED ON: CYPRESS HILL (1991)

CHORUS
Here is something you can't understand
[Sen Dog]
How I could just kill a man (x3)
[Be-Real]
Here is something you can't understand
('What does it all mean?')
[Sen Dog]
How I could just kill a man (x2)

[Sen Dog]
I been doin' all the dumb shit, yo,
Because I bet it's comin' from it
I'm not gonna waste no time, fuckin' around
like I got ya hummin'
Hummin'... comin' at cha
And you know I had to gat ya.

[Be-Real]
Time for some action, just a fraction of friction
I got the clearance to run the interference
into your satellite
Shinin' a battle light, swing out the gat
And I know that will gat ya right.
Here's an example, just a little sample.

No, I think you play like a thug
Next hear the shot of a magnum slug
Hummin', comin' at cha
Yeah, ya know I'm gonna gat ya
How you know where I'm at when you haven't
been where I've been?
Understand where I'm coming from
When you're up on the hill, in your big home
I'm out here, risking my dome
Just for a bucket, or a fast ducat
Just to stay alive
Ai, I gotta say 'Fuck it'.

[Chorus]

All I wanted was a Pepsi...

Words & Music by Larry Muggerud, Louis Freeze,
Senen Reyes, Lowell Fulson & Jimmy McCracklin

One, two, three and to the fo
Snoop Doggy Dogg and Dr Dre is at the do'
Ready to make an entrance, so back on up
(Dre: Cos you know we're bout to rip shit up)
Gimme the microphone first, so I can bust
like a bubble
Compton and Long Beach together, now you
know you in trouble
Ain't nuttin' but a G thang, baby!
Two loc'ed out niggaz so we're crazy!
Death Row is the label that pays me!
Unfadeable, so please don't try to fade this
(Hell yeah!).

But uhh, back to the lecture at hand
Perfection is perfected, so I'ma let 'em understand
From a young G's perspective
And before me dig out a bitch I have to
find a contraceptive
You never know she could be earnin' her

So sit back, relax, and strap on your seatbelt
You never been on a ride like this befo'
With a producer who can rap and control
the maestro
At the same time with the dope rhyme that I kick
You know, and I know, I flow some ol' funky shit
To add to my collection
The selection symbolises dope
Take a toke, but don't choke
If you do, you'll have no clue
On what me and my homey Snoop Dogg
came to do.

[Dre and Snoop]
It's like this and like that and like this and uh
It's like that and like this and like that and uh
It's like this.

[Dre]
And who gives a fuck about those?

DR DRE

NUTHIN' BUT A "G" THANG

RELEASED: 1992. INCLUDED ON: THE CHRONIC (1992)

man and learnin' her man
And at the same time burnin' her man
Now you know I ain't with that shit, Lieutenant
Ain't no pussy good enough to get burnt
while I'm up in it (yeah!)
And that's realer than Real-Deal Holyfield
And now you hookers and hoes know how I feel
Well if it's good enough to get broke off a
proper chunk
I'll take a small piece of some of that funky stuff.

[Dre and Snoop]
It's like this and like that and like this
And uh – it's like that and like this and like that
And uh – it's like this and like that and like this
and uh.

[Snoop]
Dre, creep to the mic like a phantom.

[Dre]
Well I'm peepin', and I'm creepin', and I'm creepin'
But I damn near got caught, cos my
beeper kept beepin'
Now it's time for me to make my impression felt

[Snoop]
So just chill, till the next episode
Fallin' back on that ass, with a hellafied
gangsta lean
Getting' funky on the mic like a old batch
of collard greens
It's the capital S, oh yes I'm fresh,
N double-O P D O double-G Y, D O
double-G, ya see
Showin' much flex when it's time to wreck a mic
Pimpin' hoes and clockin' a grip like my
name was Dolomite
Yeah, and it don't quit
I think they in the mood for some
motherfuckin' G shit (Hell yeah!)
So Dre (Whattup Dogg?) Gotta give em
what they want (What's that, G?)
We gotta break 'em off somethin' (Hell yeah!)
And it's gotta be bumpin' (City of Compton!).

[Dre]
It's where it takes place so when asked, yo' attention
Mobbin' like a muthafucker, but I ain't lynchin'
Droppin' the funky shit that's makin' the sucka
niggaz mumble

When I'm on the mic, it's like a cookie,
they all crumble
Try to get close, and your ass'll get smacked
My motherfuckin' homie Doggy Dogg has
got my back
Never let me slip, cos if I slip, then I'm slippin'
But if I got my Nina, then you know
I'm straight trippin'
And I'ma continue to put the rap down,
put the mack down
And if you bitches talk shit, I'll have
to put the smack down
Yeah, and you don't stop
I told you I'm just like a clock when
I tick and I tock
But I'm never off, always on, to the break of dawn
C-O-M-P-T-O-N, and the city they call Long Beach
Puttin' the shit together
Like my nigga D.O.C., no-one
can do it better.

[Dre and Snoop]
Like this, that and this
and uh
It's like that and like this
and like that and uh
It's like this.

[Dre]
And who gives a
fuck about those?

[Snoop]
So just chill,
till the next
episode

*Words & Music by
Calvin Broadus, Leon
Haywood & Frederick Knight
© Copyright 1993
Suge Publishing/WB Music
Corporation/Music Corporation
of America Incorporated/
Jim-Edd Music/Two-Knight
Publishing Company/
Irving Music Incorporated, USA.
Warner/Chappell Music Limited,
Griffin House (50%)/
Universal/MCA Music Limited (40%)/
Rondor Music (London) Limited (10%).
All Rights Reserved.
International Copyright Secured.*

DR DRE...

The impact of Andre Young's productions in the 90s has been compared by some to Phil Spector's 60s output. Although there is little basis for sonic comparison, each was midwife to a musical idea that came to dominate an era. Where Spector's wall of sound gave a new acoustic space for girl groups to flourish in, Dre's G-Funk aesthetic encompassed lumbering beats, honey-thick bass lines, single-note keyboard embellishments and arresting, often astonishing samples. Though DJ Premier of Gang Starr, Marley Marl of the Juice Crew, Public Enemy's Bomb Squad and the Wu-Tang's RZA hold greater claims as true production innovators, none achieved the aural dominance of a genre that Dre enjoyed in the early 90s.

For all the plaudits afforded his work on the boards, Dre is not one of rap's great MCs. His thick-vowelled flow, like his lyrics, is too often a blunt instrument on record. Which is why he's teamed up with a coterie of collaborators since his early days in N.W.A. Although he has made stunning records in conjunction with N.W.A. (he and Ice Cube gelled particularly well) and later Eminem, his greatest partnership was forged with protégé Snoop Doggy Dogg, the laconic Long Island rapper he discovered.

Dre's debut album was always destined to make waves, but its global impact shook even its author as it stayed in the American top 10 for some eight months. 'Nuthin' But A "G" Thang', a Top 10 single, was *The Chronic*'s defining moment. Snoop's elastic larynx and Dre's instinct for re-imagining old soul hooks mixed a priceless cocktail. As they boasted in the opening stanza, 'Compton and Long Beach together, now you know you in trouble!' Snoop makes the track with his lachrymose enunciation and distinctive, end-of-line hooks (and catch the reference to collard greens, the soul food staple first mentioned in The Sugarhill Gang's 'Rapper's Delight' and Run D-M-C's 'Sucker MCs').

'Nuthin' But A "G" Thang' was a honey-coated expansion on N.W.A.'s more theatrical firestorm of sound – with a dominant bass motif as well as childlike electronica cooking up the 'funky shit' acknowledged in the lyrics. 'G Thang' was conceived as a lifestyle track and expresses what would become typical gangsta sentiments. Offering reportage rather than editorial, its listless diarists document their immediate environment with something approaching disinterest.

SNOOP DOGGY DOGG...

Calvin Broadus, a former gang-affiliated drug dealer from Long Beach, is the gentleman assassin of gangsta rap, a lean, poodle-featured sophisti-cat serving up lyrics revelling in gruesomely violent imagery. He served his apprenticeship as part of the 213 trio, alongside later G-Funk stars Warren G and Nate Dogg. One of their demos reached N.W.A. alumnus Dr. Dre, who immediately used Snoop on 'Deep Cover'. Then came a show-stealing guest spot on Dre's multi-million selling *The Chronic* where Snoop fought off tough opposition to prove himself Death Row's top dog MC.But like many gangsta rappers, Snoop found it difficult to differentiate between the fiction of his records and real life. Having already served time for drugs offences, he came close to lasting incarceration after his involvement in the murder of a LA gang member by his bodyguard. The humbled Snoop was pictured cowed in prayer in court, but the incident was a media godsend – it set his credentials up nicely for his solo debut, *Doggystyle*.

Doggystyle became the fastest selling debut in history. With production handled by gangsta rap's beatmeister Dr Dre, the album, with its insouciant, carefree spectre of violence and Snoop's wantonly misanthropic asides, delivered in large parts on its promise. Despite the boasts about despatching his enemies and some frankly villainous portrayals of women, there was a warmth and charm to the contents that recalled Slick Rick, but also established Snoop's own charismatic, somehow redeemable persona. He became the biggest rap star of the early 90s, the 'number one G' of the G-Funk (or gangsta-funk) era. Although many of his lyrics glorified marijuana use (or 'the chronic'), it was a cinematic alcohol eulogy, 'Gin And Juice', that became the album's biggest single. Collaborator Nate Dogg recalled that the song was essentially improvised: 'He just got on the mic and said what he had to say.' The track, which featured additional vocals from Dogg Pound associate Dat Nigga Daz, had the dubious honour of introducing the world to Snoop's 'beeyatch!' catchphrase.

Post-*Doggystyle* Snoop's career declined as the legendary Death Row records dissolved in acrimony and blood-letting. Bereft of Dre's master touch a second album, *Tha Doggfather*, offered only tantalising glimpses of former glories. Snoop is still out there, though his profile has diminished since he was public enemy number one in 1993.

[Sound of urinating]

[Dre]
Ai baby, ai baby
Ai baby, get some bubblegum in this motherfucker
Steady long, steady long nigga.

[Snoop]
With so much drama in the L-B-C
It's kinda hard bein' Snoop D-O-double-G
But I, somehow, some way
Keep comin' up with funky-ass shit
like every single day
May I kick a little something for the G's? (yeah)
And make a few ends as (yeah!) I breeze, through?
Two in the mornin' and the party's still jumpin'
Cos my momma ain't home
I got bitches in the living room getting' it on
And they ain't leavin' til six in the mornin'
(six in the mornin')

Eighty degrees, when I tell that bitch please
Raise up off these N-U-T's, cos you gets
none of these
At ease.
As I mob with the Dogg Pound, feel the breeze
Beeyatch, I'm just –

Rollin' down the street, smokin' indo'
Sippin' on gin and juice
Laid back (with my mind on my money
and my money on my mind) (x2).

Later on that day my homey Dr. Dre came
through with a gang of Tanqueray
And a fat ass J, of some bubonic chronic
that made me choke
Shit, this ain't no joke
I had to back up off of it
And sit my cup down
Tanqueray and chronic, yeah I'm fucked up now

SNOOP DOGGY DOGG

GIN AND JUICE

RELEASED 1993: INCLUDED ON: DOGGYSTYLE (1993)

So what you wanna do, sheet I got a pocket full
of rubbers and my homeboys do too
So turn off the lights and close the doors
But (but what) we don't love them hoes, yeah!
So we gonna smoke a ounce to this G's up,
hoes down
While you motherfuckers bounce to this.

Rollin down the street, smokin' indo'
Sippin' on gin and juice
Laid back (with my mind on my money and
my money on my mind) (x2).

Now that I got me some Seagram's gin
Everybody got they cups, but they ain't chipped in
Now this types of shit happens all the time
You got to get yours but fool I gotta get mine
Everything is fine when you listenin' to the D-O-G
I got the cultivating music that be captivating he
Who listens to the words that I speak
As I take me a drink to the middle of the street
And get to mackin' to this bitch named
Sadie (Sadie?)
She used to be the homeboy's lady (Oh, that bitch)

But it ain't no stoppin', I'm still poppin'
Dre got some bitches from the city of Compton
To serve me, not with a cherry on top
Cos when I bust my nut, I'm raisin' up off the cot
Don't get upset girl, that's just how it goes
I don't love you hoes, I'm out the do'
And I'll be –

Rollin' down the street, smokin' indo'
Sippin' on gin and juice (beeyatch!)
Laid back (with my mind on my money and my
money on my mind) (x2).

Words & Music by Calvin Broadus, Andre Young, Mark Adams,
Raymond Turner, Daniel Webster, Stephen Washington,
Steve Arrington, Harry Casey & Richard Finch
© *Copyright 1992 Cotillion Music Incorporated / Suge Publishing /*
WB Music Corporation / Longitude Music Company / Sony /
ATV Tunes LLC, USA.
Warner / Chappell Music Limited, Griffin House,
161 Hammersmith Road, London W6 8BS (70%) / Peermusic (UK)
Limited, 8-14 Verulam Street, London WC1X 8LZ (25%) /
Sony / ATV Music Publishing (UK) Limited,
10 Great Marlborough Street, London W1F 7LP (5%).

[Raekwon the Chief and Method Man]
What that nigga want, God?
Word up, look out for the cops
[Wu-Tang five finger shit]
(Cash Rules)
Word up, two for fives over here baby
Word up, two for fives them niggaz got
garbage down the way
Word up, know what I'm sayin'?
(Cash Rules Everything Around Me C.R.E.A.M.)
Yeah, check this ol' fly shit out, word up
(Cash Rules Everything Around Me)
Take you on a natural joint
(C.R.E.A.M. get the money)
Here we here we go (dollar dollar bill y'all)
Check this shit, yo!

[Raekwon]
I grew up on the crime side,
the New York Times side

Staying alive was no jive
At second hands, moms bounced on old men
So then we moved to Shaolin land
A young youth, yo rockin the gold tooth
'Lo goose
Only way, I begin to gee off was drug loot
And let's start it like this son, rollin' with this one
And that one, pullin' out gats for fun
But it was just a dream for the teen,
who was a fiend
Started smokin' woolies at sixteen
And running up in gates, and doing hits
for high stakes
Making my way on fire escapes
No question I would speed, for cracks and weed
The combination made my eyes bleed
No question I would flow off, and try to
get the dough all

WU-TANG CLAN

C.R.E.A.M.

(CASH RULES EVERYTHING AROUND ME)

RELEASED: 1993. INCLUDED ON: ENTER THE WU-TANG (36 CHAMBERS) (1993)

Sticking up white boys in ball court
My life got no better, same damn 'Lo sweater
Times is rough and tough like leather
Figured out I went the wrong route
So I got with a sick-ass click and went all out
Catchin' keys from across seas
Rollin in MPV's
Every week we made forty Gs
Yo nigga respect mine, or anger the tech nine
Chck-POW! Move from the gate now.

[Method Man]
Cash Rules Everything Around Me C.R.E.A.M.
Get the money
Dollar, dollar bill y'all (x2).

[Inspector Deck]
It's been twenty-two long hard years of
still strugglin'
Survival got me buggin', but I'm alive on arrival
I peep at the shape of the streets
And stay awake to the ways of the world cos
shit is deep

A man with a dream with plans to
make C.R.E.A.M.
Which failed – I went to jail at the age of 15
A young buck sellin' drugs and such who
never had much
Trying to get a clutch at what I could not
(could not...)
The court played me short, now I face incarceration
Pacin' – going up state's my destination
Handcuffed in back of a bus, forty of us
Life as a shorty shouldn't be so rough
But as the world turns I learned life is hell
Living in the world no different from a cell
Everyday I escape from Jakes givin' chase, sellin' base
Smokin' bones in the staircase
Though I don't know why I chose to smoke sess
I guess that's the time when I'm not depressed
But I'm still depressed, and I ask what's it worth?
Ready to give up so I seek the Old Earth
Who explained working hard may
help you maintain
To learn to overcome the heartaches and pain
We got stick-up kids, corrupt cops, and
crack rocks and stray shots
All on the block that stays hot
Leave it up to me while I be living proof
To kick the truth to the young black youth
But shorty's runnin' wild smokin' sess, drinkin' beer
And ain't trying to hear what I'm kickin' in his ear
Neglected, but now, but yo, it gots to be accepted
That what? That life is hectic.

Cash Rules Everything Around Me C.R.E.A.M.
Get the money – dollar, dollar bill
Yeah! [repeat over next lines]

Niggas got to do what they gotta do, to get a bill
Ya know what I'm saying?
Cos we can't just get by no more.
Word up, we gotta get over, straight up and down.

WU-TANG CLAN...

With rap's power locus transplanted to the west coast after Dr Dre's G-Funk hybrid proved irresistible, it took a crazy-ass family of martial arts-fixated, chess-playing, Sun Tzu-quoting Staten Islanders with their own esoteric personality and identity problems to bring the props back to the Big Apple.

The Wu-Tang (modelled on the Shaolin discipline extolled in kung fu flick folklore), were built around linchpin member Robert Diggs or RZA, their house producer and founder. He'd already cut a single for Tommy Boy (as Prince Rakeem) before orchestrating the WTC's debut single, 'Protect Ya Neck', which he pressed up himself shortly after his prison release. He came up with a masterplan, forged partially from martial art philosophies, but also drawing from the Koran and I-Ching. The Wu-Tang Clan was to be an empire of art and industry – an idiosyncratic entity operating its own comic books, clothing lines and publishing. Improbably confident of his own future, RZA managed to convince Rich Isaacson at RCA Records to give the group a global contract whilst allowing each member of the clan to cut their own solo deals.

The family made its breakthrough with 1993's *Enter The Wu-Tang (36 Chambers)*, an improbable journey into paranoia, mysticism and insomnia fuelled by sparse, grimy beats that percolated through a vista of shadows and amorphous sonic currents. The contents of an album routinely credited with being the most shockingly original rap record of the 90s defied convention and logic. Despite the allusions to schizophrenically-entwined ancient philosophies, it was impossible to deny the impact of the album's keynote address, 'C.R.E.A.M. (Cash Rules Everything Around Me)'. More than just craven capitalism, it offered a bleak rationale for the group's mindset and also witnessed the consummate Wu-Tang collaborative performance. Its sentiments took listeners back to EPMD's 'getting paid' ethos but set it in a new world of increasing desperation populated by cut-throat survivalists. Following *36 Chambers* the collective has produced a roll call of platinum and multi-platinum solo albums. The group's second album proper, *Wu-Tang Forever*, was a vast disappointment, but they remain a force, even if some of their mythic invincibility looks to have worn as thin as the indefatigable Ol' Dirty Bastard's prison report card.

Nigga, you need to git up, git out and git somethin'
Don't let the days of your life pass by
You need to git up, git out and git somethin'
Don't spend all your time tryin' to get high
You need to git up, git out and git somethin'
How will you make it if you never even try?
You need to git up, git out and git somethin'
Cos you and I got to do for you and I.

[Cee-Lo]
I don't recall, ever graduatin' at all
Sometimes I feel I'm just a disappointment to y'all
Every day, I just lay around then I can't be found
Always asked to give me some livin' life like a bum
Times is rough, my auntie got enough
problems of her own

Cos every job I get is cruel and demeanin'
Sick of takin trash out and toilet bowl cleanin'
But I'm also sick and tired of strugglin'
I never ever thought I'd have resort to
drug smugglin'
Naw, that ain't what I'm about
Cee-lo will just continue travelling this route
Without any doubt or fear
I know the Lord ain't brought me this far
So he could drop me off here
Did I make myself clear?

Nigga, you need to git up, git out and git somethin'
Don't let the days of your life pass by
You need to git up, git out and git somethin'
Don't spend all your time tryin to get high
You need to git up, git out and git somethin'
How will you make it if you never even try?
You need to git up, git out and git somethin'

OUTKAST
GIT UP, GIT OUT
(FEATURING THE GOODIE MOB)
RELEASED: 1994. INCLUDED ON SOUTHERNPLAYALISTICADILLACMUZIK (1994)

Nigga, you supposed to be grown!
I agree, I try to be the man I'm 'posed to be
But negativity is all you seem to ever see
I admit, I've done some dumb shit
And I'm probably gonna do some mo'
You shouldn't hold that against me, though
Why not? My music's all that I got
But some time must be contested for this
to be manifested
I know you know but I'm gonna say this to you
I get high – but I don't get too high
So what's the limit 'posed to be?
That must be why you can't get your ass up
out the bed before three
You need to git up, git out, cut that bullshit out
Ain't you sick and tired of having to do without?
And what up with all these questions?
As act as though you know somethin' I don't
Do you have any suggestions?

Cos you and I got to do for you and I.

[Big Boi]
Well, git up, stand up.
So what's said, you dickhead?
See when I was a youngsta, used to
wear them fuckin' Pro Keds
My mama made me do it, but the devil,
he made me smart
Told me to jack them weak ass niggaz
for they fuckin' Starters
In the middle school, I was a bigger fool
I wore with tank tops to show off my tattoo
Thought I was cool
I used to hang out with my daddy's brothers,
I call them my uncles
They taught me how to smoke herb,
I followed them when they ran numbers
So in a sense I was Rosemary's baby
And then, I learned the difference between
a bitch and a lady
Hell, I treat 'em all like hoes, see I pimped 'em

Bitch never had my money, so I never whipped 'em
See all the playas came and all the playas went
A playa ain't a gangsta but a playa can
handle his shit bitch
You need to git up, git out, git somethin'
Smoke out, cos it's all about money, money, money
Yeah I said it, a nigga sportin' plats and a Braves' hat
I hang with Rico Wade cos the Dungeon
is where the funk's at
Boy I'm true to Organized, cos they raised me
I'm also down with LaFace, cos L.A. Reid,
yeah, he pays me
And it's cool Yeah, it's real cool
Getting' paid fat pockets and all that other
phat shit like that

Ha! Ha!

Nigga, you need to git up, git out and git somethin'
Don't let the days of your life pass by
You need to git up, git out and git somethin'
Don't spend all your time tryin to get high
You need to git up, git out and git somethin'
How will you make it if you never even try?
You need to git up, git out and git somethin'
Cos you and I got to do for you and I.

[Big Gipp]
A lot of people in my past tried to do me, screw me
Throw me over in the fire, let me get
chunky and charred
Like a piece of wood and dem spirits
got the mutant's mind

I'm gettin paranoid and steady lookin' for the time
It's eight in the mornin' and ain't nobody up yet
I got my long johns, get my coat and throw
on my ball cap
I'm headed out the door, to get off in my ride
I'm diggin through the ashtray, hopin' to
have a good day
I had Jamaica's best and when I light it up,
I hear a voice in my head
(You got to git up, git out and git somethin')
Now I know it's on, my day is finally started
Back up in my crib, eat my shit, break out quick
In my slick '84 Sedan DeVille
Steady bouncin', out the Pointe to Cambelton Road
The valley of the Southside flow
Everybody know about that killa that we call blow
So keep your eyes peeled for the 'cover unit
Cos they known for jumpin' out of black
Chevy trucks and through the fog
Here come the Red Dogs, I'm bustin'
out around the corner in my hog
Dippin' from the area, I'm scared
So one of these bitches might wind up dead
Cos I have no time for bail
Fuck Clampett cops. Fuck Elgin Bail
And crooked ass Jackson, got the
whole country thinkin'
That my city is the big lick for '96, '94
Big Gipp, Goodie Mo, Outkast
A vision from the past
Hootie Hoo - my white owls are burnin'
kinda slow.

Nigga, you need to git up, git out and git somethin'
Don't let the days of your life pass by
You need to git up, git out and git somethin'
Don't spend all your time tryin' to get high
You need to git up, git out and git somethin'
How will you make it if you never even try?
You need to git up, git out and git somethin'
Cos you and I got to do for you and I.

[Dre]
Y'all tellin me that I need to get out and vote, huh?
Why? Ain't nobody black runnin' but crackers
So, why I got to register?
I thinkin' of better shit to do with my time
Never smelled aroma of diploma,
but I write the deep ass rhymes
So let me take ya way back to when
a nigga stayed in South west Atlanta
Y'all could not tell me nuthin', thought
I hit that bottom rock

At age 13, start workin' at the loading dock
They layin' my mama off of work,
General Motors trippin'
But I come home Bank like Hank, from
lickin' and dippin'
Doin' dumb shit, not knowin' what
a nigga know now
Yeah, that petty shit will have you
cased up and locked down
I dips, over to East Point, still actin' a fool
Wastin' my time in the school, I'd rather
be shootin' pool
Cool is how I played the tenth grade
I thought it was all about mackin' hoes
and wearin' pimp fade
Instead of bein' in class, I'd rather be up in some ass
Not, thinkin' about them six courses
that I need to pass
Graduation rolled around like rolly-pollies
Damn, that's fucked up
I shoulda listened when my mama told me
That, if you play now, you gonna suffer later
Figured she was talkin' yang-yang,
so I paid her no attention
And kept missin' the point she tried
to poke me with
The doper that I get, the more I'm feelin'
broke and shit
Huh, but that don't matter though,
I am an O-UT-KAST
So get up off your ass.

Nigga, you need to git up, git out and git somethin'
Don't let the days of your life pass by
You need to git up, git out and git somethin'
Don't spend all your time tryin' to get high
You need to git up, git out and git somethin'
How will you make it if you never even try?
You need to git up, git out and git somethin'
Cos you and I got to do for you and I

You need to... (repeat till fade)

Words & Music by Antwan Patton, Andre Benjamin,
Thomas Burton, Cameron Gipp, Rico Wade,
Patrick Brown & Raymon Murray

OUTKAST...

The deep fried funk and world-weary wit of southern drawlers Andre 'Dre' Benjamin and Antwan 'Big Boi' Patton has been one of rap's saving graces in the 90s. While others spluttered inanities about 'keeping it real' then waxed lyrical about mowing down lines of policemen as if they were extras from *Zulu*, OutKast were donning wigs, breeding dogs and taking risks. By far the most captivating exponents of the dirty south's 'bling bling' culture of living large and dressing fine, they bounced from politics to partying without missing a beat and offered a welcome distraction from the unhinged rivalry between the west and east coast rap enclaves.

They didn't just eschew the herd mentality when it came to music. While Big Boi is southern homeboy incarnate in jeans and gridiron sportswear, Dre is an exhibitionist of some standing, a vision in blonde wigs and pink fur. While everybody else was ripping off George Clinton's back catalogue, until Outkast no-one had really considered aping his wardrobe. Taken from their 1994 debut album, 'Git Up, Git Out' was an ode to self-belief and fighting the good fight amid the blaxploitation, sci-fi, pimpin' and Cadillac-cruising tales. Unlike their peers, most notably Master P's stable of gangsta rappers, OutKast could sketch the details while avoiding the worst clichés of the southern 'playa' lifestyle – ensuring that they could pull off something that read like a self-help guide without sounding either preachy or dull.

Released on Babyface's LaFace Records, the album boasted the production skills of Organized Noise. Their tough, G-funk-derived beats were enlivened by live instruments with an audible southern twang – the perfect match for Big Boi and Dre's cushioned flow.

From this flying start OutKast have gone on to produce such thematically and sonically diverse efforts as *ATLiens* (1996) and *Aquemini* (1998), each showcasing intricate lyrics, dense musical textures and scoopfuls of goofy humour. By the time Benjamin had become Andre 3000, they delivered a new milestone in *Stankonia* (2000), a triple platinum success featuring the number one pop single 'Ms Jackson'. It provided further evidence that the future of southern hip hop is safe in the custody of this likeable odd couple, who have been dropping science for years without ever creating anything that wasn't a hoot to listen to.

TUPAC SHAKUR...

Tupac Shakur represented perfectly the posturing, contradictions and internal feuding of 90s rap music. While his career provides a ghoulish spectacle there is also a genuine sense of loss and waste. His life was ended by a moment in which the street-level vendettas played out on rap records suddenly became terrifyingly real. Tupac rapped about his impending demise with such conviction it is hard not to read some of his lyrics as an extended suicide note.

By the time of his death Tupac had become the dominant figure in rap music and a mainstream film star. Yet his origins were far different to those suggested by his fast-track self-martyrdom and the legendary 'Thug Life' tattoo that adorned his arm. As a child, any wrongdoing resulted in his mother forcing him to read an entire copy of the *New York Times*. He subsequently studied ballet at the Baltimore School for the Arts before taking a side part with Bay Area eccentrics Digital Underground. His solo bow, 1991's *2Pacalypse Now*, balanced pleas for the civil rights agenda against blood-curdling cynicism. The subsequent *Strictly 4 My N.I.G.G.A.Z.* and *Me Against The World* declined into aggressive misanthropy, though Tupac was always capable of leavening the onslaught of threats and boasts with selective bouts of conscience.

By the time he cut the fatalistic *All Eyez On Me* the clock was ticking on Tupac's life. Having already survived one murder attempt he had spent close on a year in jail, brooding and scheming. The sprawling double set was recorded in a matter of days after he'd been sprung from prison by Death Row's Suge Knight. But amid the inconsistency were gems such as 'California Love', which b-sided his 1997 number one 'How Do U Want It'. Amid the slew of inflammatory tracks ricocheting between west and east coasts, Tupac occupied an interesting position – though born in New York, his loyalties belonged resolutely to the west coast. This eulogy to his adopted state was a celebration of the Californian hip hop lifestyle rather than an attempt to diss New Yorker rappers.

Tupac's appeal always rested on the mythology of the man more than his music, and the fact that the dramatic events he chronicled in his lyrics paled in comparison to the actuality of his own existence. He was a far better actor, in real life *and* on the screen, than he ever was an MC. Tupac Shakur was shot dead in September 1996 in Las Vegas.

California love!
California – knows how to party
California – knows how to party
In the city of L.A.
In the city of good ol' Watts
In the city, the city of Compton
We keep it rockin'! We keep it rockin'!

[Dr Dre]
Now let me welcome everybody to the
wild, wild west
A state that's untouchable like Elliot Ness
The track hits ya eardrum like a slug to ya chest
Pack a vest for your Jimmy in the city of sex
We in that sunshine state with a bomb
ass hemp beat
The state where ya never find a dance floor empty
And pimps be on a mission for them greens
Lean mean money-makin'-machines servin' fiends
I been in the game for ten years makin' rap tunes
Ever since honeys was wearin' sassoon
Now it's '95 and they clock me and watch me
Diamonds shinin', lookin' like I robbed Liberace
It's all good, from Diego to tha Bay
Your city is tha bomb if your city makin' pay
Throw up a finger if ya feel the same way
Dre puttin' it down for Californ-i-a.

California – knows how to party
California – knows how to party
In the city of L.A.
In the city of good ol' Watts
In the city, the city of Compton
We keep it rockin'! We keep it rockin'!
Shake it, shake it baby
Shake it, shake it baby
Shake it, shake it mama
Shake it Cali
Shake it, shake it baby
Shake it, shake it, shake it, shake it.

[2Pac]
Out on bail, fresh out of jail,
California dreamin'
Soon as I step on the scene,
I'm hearin' hoochies screamin'
Fiendin' for money and alcohol
The life of a Westside player where
cowards die and the strong ball
Only in Cali, where we riot not rally
To live and die in L.A.
We wearin' Chucks not Ballies
(yeah, that's right)
Dressed in Locs and khaki suits and
ride is what we do

Flossin' but have caution, we collide
with other crews
Famous because we throw grands
Worldwide let 'em recognise from Long Beach
to Rosecranz
Bumpin' and grindin' like a slow jam
It's Westside so you know the Row won't
bow down to no man
Say what you say, but give me that
bomb beat from Dre
Let me serenade the streets of L.A.
From Oakland to Sac-town, the Bay Area
and back down
Cali is where they put they mack down,
give me love!
California – knows how to party
California – knows how to party
In the city of L.A.
In the city of good ol' Watts
In the city, the city of Compton
We keep it rockin'! We keep it rockin'!

[Dre]
Now make it shake!
Shake it, shake it baby
Shake it, shake it baby
Shake it, shake it mama
Shake it Cali
Shake it, shake it baby
Shake it, shake it, shake it, shake it.

[Dre & 2Pac]
Uh, yeah, uh, Long Beach in tha house
Uh yeah, Oaktown, Oakland definitely in
tha house, ha-ha-ha
Frisco, Frisco.

[2Pac]
Hey, you know LA is up in this Pasadena,
where you at, yeah?
Ingelwood, Ingelwood always up
to no good
Even Hollywood tryin' to get a piece, baby

TUPAC SHAKUR
CALIFORNIA LOVE
RELEASED: 1996. INCLUDED ON: ALL EYEZ ON ME (1996)

Sacramento, Sacramento where ya at?
Yeah, throw it up y'all, throw it up
Throw it up
Let's show these fools how
we do this on that west side
Cause you and I know it's tha best side,
yeah.
That's right,
West coast, west coast, uh
California love
California love.

*Words & Music by Tupac Shakur, Andre
Young, Roger Troutman, Larry Troutman,
Joe Cocker, Chris Stainton,
Mikel Hooks & Ronnie Hudson*

© *Copyright 1996 Songs Of Lastrada/
Saja Music Company/Delirious
Music/Embassy Music Corporation/
Sony/ATV Songs LLC, USA.
Onward Music Ltd. (40%)/Sony/ATV
Music Publishing (UK) Ltd. (35%)/
Campbell Connelly & Company Ltd.
(25%). All Rights Reserved.
International Copyright Secured.*

Bad Boy... we ain't gonna stop.

[Ma$e]
Now with Sean on the hot track,
melt like it's hot wax
Put it out, all the stores, bet you could
shop that (that's right)
Leave a nigga with a hot hat, fronting like
Bad Boy ain't got tracks (nigga stop that)
There's no guy slicker than this young fly nigga
Nickel-nine nigga, floss, you die quicker (uh-huh)
This fed time outta town pie flipper
Turn Cristal into a crooked I sipper
Everbody want to be fast, see the cash
Fuck around they weak staff, get a heat rash
Anything in Bad Boy way we smash (we smash)
Hundred G stash, push a bulletproof E-Class
(heh heh)

I'm through with bein' a player and a baller
Just want me one bad bitch so I can spoil her
Ma$e wanna be the one you respect
Even when you're vexed
Rock Versace silks over spilled brunette
Got green never seen so you suck my jewels
Clutch my Uz', anything I touch I bruise
Puff make his own laws, nigga fuck your rules
(that's right)
Goodfellas, you know you can't touch us dudes.

[Puff]
Don't push us, cos we're close to the edge
We're tryin' not to lose our heads, a-ha ha ha.

[Mase]
Broken glass everywhere [sound of glass shattering]
If it ain't about the money, Puff, I just don't care
(that's right)
I'm that Goodfella fly guy, sometimes wiseguys

PUFF DADDY
CAN'T NOBODY HOLD ME DOWN
RELEASED: 1997. INCLUDED ON: NO WAY OUT (1997)

Spend time in H-A-W-A-I-I
(Ma$e can you please stop smoking la-la?)
Puff, why try? I'm a thug, I'ma die high
I be out in Jersey, puffin' Hershey Brothers
Ain't worthy to rock my derby
Though I'm never drugged, I'm the venom in
the club, G
Though I know the thug be wantin' to slug me
(uh-huh)
Could it be I move as smooth as Bugsy? (yeah)
Or be at the bar with too much bubbly? (c'mon)
Yo I think it must be the girls want to lust me
Or is it simply the girls just love me?
Brothers wanna rock the Rolls, rock my clothes
Rock my ice, pull out Glocks, stop my life (uhh)
I'm like, 'Damn, how these niggaz got they trust?
Used to be my man, how you gonna plot
on my wife?'
Do you think you snake me, cos they hate me?
Or he got his Ph.D; Player Hater's Degree? (Aha!)

[Together]
[Ma$e]
Can't nobody take my pride

[Puff] Uh-uh, uh-uh
[Ma$e] Can't nobody hold me down... oh no
[Ma$e] I got to keep on movin'.

[Puff]
Quit that! (uh-huh)
You a big cat? (yeah)
Where your chicks at? (yeah)
Where your whips at? (where dey at?)
Wherever you get stacks, I'm'a fix that
Everything that's big dreams, I did that (that's right)
Don't knock me cos you're boring
I'm record sales soaring, straight touring
Simply a lot of men be wantin' to hear me
Cos their words just don't offend me (uh-uh, uh-uh)
We spend cheese, in the West Indies
Then come home to plenty cream Bentleys (aha!)
You name it, I could claim it
Young, black, and famous, with money
hangin' out the anus
And when you need a hit, who you go and get?
(who?)
Bet against us? (Not a sure bet)
We make hits that'll rearrange your whole set
(that's right)
And got a Benz that I ain't even drove yet.

[Ma$e]
Don't push us, cos we're close to the edge
We're tryin' not to lose our heads, a-ha-ha-ha-ha
I get the feeling sometimes it makes me wonder
Why you wanna take us under
[Puff]
Why you wanna take us under
Why you wanna take us under.

[Together]
[Ma$e]
Can't nobody take my pride
[Puff] Uh-uh, uh-uh
[Ma$e] Can't nobody hold me down... oh no
[Ma$e] I got to keep on movin'.

PUFF DADDY...

The karaoke king of rap, the career of Puff Daddy (going under the moniker of P. Diddy these days) offers conclusive proof that talent need be no impediment to massive international success. But to be fair to a man who is as reviled in hip hop circles as Delores Tucker or Charlton Heston, he has a good business brain and, prior to his entrance on the world music scene, nobody dreamed they could stretch so little so far.

Sean 'Puffy' Combs' ascent began while attending college at Howard University in Washington, where he promoted parties till friend Heavy D secured him an intern's job at Andre Harrell's Uptown Records. He quickly proved his A&R skills by piloting the breakthrough of new jack swingers Jodeci and Mary J. Blige. But when he set up his own Bad Boy Entertainment imprint while still in the employ of Uptown, and got fired for his troubles, it was time to see if his own colossal self-belief was justified.

In a business sense, it was. He took Bad Boy to Arista Records and success continued unabated in 1994 with Craig Mack's *Flava In Ya Ear* and the late Notorious B.I.G.'s *Ready To Die*. Combs also attempted to corner the R&B market with releases from Biggie's wife Faith Evans and Total. As well as the usual rap mogul madness of setting up clothes brands and the like, and stamping executive producer over everything that came out of Bad Boy, Puff Daddy hankered for his own turn in the spotlight. Hence *No Way Out*, released in 1997, which included his Police-sampling, mawkish tribute to Biggie, 'I'll Be Missing You'. Not much of a singer, and certainly not much of a rapper, it didn't prevent the song from topping the charts on both sides of the Atlantic and pushing its parent album to seven-times platinum sales. 'Can't Nobody Hold Me Down', rapped by Ma$e, Bad Boy's biggest MC post-Biggie, with Puffy safely confined to chorus duties, was the other big single from the album – an unapologetic Bad Boy brag-fest featuring the sparkling line 'Young, black, and famous, with money hangin' out the anus'. This time the sample was Grandmaster Flash's 'The Message' (though describing this as a sample disguises the fact that rather than employ an illustrative hook it fillets the original wholesale). Thereafter Combs has become embroiled in tabloid gossip, celebrity relationships and legal problems. With any luck it might be years before his schedule allows him anywhere near a studio again.

MISSY ELLIOTT...

The tradition of female MCs in hip hop,
Salt-N-Pepa aside, has too often been one of
instant success followed by enforced silence.
But where Yo Yo, Monie Love and the various
Roxannes saw their careers tail off, and while
Queen Latifah defected to sitcoms and Lauryn Hill
has been rebranded as a soul singer, hip hop may
have found a female star with longevity in the
vibrant presence of Missy 'Misdemeanor' Elliott.

Native Virginian Elliott started out as a singer in
the teenage R&B act Sista, securing her first
recording deal after auditioning for DeVante Swing
from Jodeci. She was devastated when Sista's
debut flopped, but responded by composing songs
for artists including Jodeci and Aaliyah and guest-
rapping on releases by MC Lyte and SWV. It was
rumoured that the reason it took her so long to
find a home for her debut album was due to
disinterested labels focusing on more photogenic
artists, keeping Elliott working in the background.
However, Elliott is a tough cookie, and a persistent
one, as Elektra execs can testify after they signed
her on the proviso that she'd be allowed to
organise her own music division.

Her transition to rapping MC with full-flavoured
R&B vocals was in full effect by the release of
Supa Dupa Fly, her 1997 debut album. It included
contributions from Da Brat and Lil' Kim as well as
close friend Aaliyah. Other guests included Busta
Rhymes and Ginuwine (for whom she had also
written hits). The marriage of R&B, new age hip
hop and Elliott's exuberant vocal interludes,
underpinned by the clinical production of fellow
Virginian Timbaland, was instantly appealing.
Through a series of classy videos she began to
gain support from MTV and other networks,
wrongfooting those who'd insisted she should
avoid visual media. The album quickly went double
platinum and earned her a Grammy nomination.
'The Rain' also made a legend of Timbaland's
compelling but strangely impersonal digital funk.
Precise, synthetic and minimalist, the liquid sheen
that Timbaland applied to Elliott's debut would
soon be extended to releases by Jay-Z, Nas and
Snoop Dogg. Just like the Sugar Hill house band
two decades earlier, these tracks were cut without
the use of samples and relied on Timbaland's own
instrumentation instead (ironically 'The Rain' was
the only song on *Supa Dupa Fly* to include a
sample, in this case Ann Pebbles' original version
of 'I Can't Stand The Rain').

Me I'm supa fly (uh-huh)
Supa dupa fly (uh-huh)
Supa dupa fly
I can't stand the rain!
Me I'm supa fly (uh-huh)
'gainst my window (x3).

When the rain hits my window
I take in [cough and inhale] me some indo
Me and Timbaland, ooh, we sang a jangle
We so tight, that you get our styles tangled
Sway on dosie-do like you loco
(Can we get kinky tonight?)
Like CoCo – so-so
You don't wanna play with my yo-yo
I smoke my hydro on the dee-low.

I can't stand the rain! (uh-huh, uh-huh)
'gainst my window (against my window) (x3)
I can't stand the rain! (uh-huh, uh-huh)
'gainst my window (say what?).

I got my umbrella
My finger waves be dazed, they fall like
Humpty Chumpy
I break up with him before he dump me
To have me, yes you lucky.

I can't stand the rain! (uh-huh)
'gainst my window (uh-huh)
I can't stand the rain! (uh-huh, uh-huh)
'gainst my window (against my window)
I can't stand the rain! (uh-huh)
'gainst my window (what?)
I can't stand the rain! (uh-huh)
'gainst my window (uh)
I can't stand the rain! (what?) (I like that baby)
I can't stand the rain! (can you stand the rain?)
(uh-huh, stand the rain)
I can't stand the rain! (what?)
(can you stand the rain?)
I can't stand the rain! (can you stand the rain?)
(uh-huh, can you stand the rain?)

MISSY 'MISDEMEANOR' ELLIOTT

THE RAIN (SUPA DUPA FLY)

RELEASED: 1997. INCLUDED ON: SUPA DUPA FLY (1997)

Yeah. Beep beep, who got the keys to the Jeep?
Vroooom! (uh-huh) I'm drivin' to the beach
Top down, loud sounds, see my peeps (uhh)
Give them pounds, now look who it be (who it be)
It be me me, me and Timothy (me me!)
Look like it's 'bout to rain, what a shame (uh-huh)
I got the Armor-All to shine up the stain
Oh Missy, try to maintain
Icky-icky-icky-icky-icky.

I can't stand the rain! (uh-huh, uh-huh)
I can't stand the rain! (say what? uh-huh, uh-huh)
'gainst my window (uh-huh)
I can't stand the rain! (uh-huh, uh-huh)
'gainst my window (x2)
I can't stand the rain!

I feel the wind
Five six seven, eight nine ten
Begin
I sit on Hill's like Lauryn
Until the rain starts, comin'
down, pourin' – Chill

I can't stand the rain! (what?)
'gainst my window (uh-huh)
I can't stand the rain!
'gainst my window (huh)
I can't stand the rain! (hmmm)
'gainst my window (yo)
I can't stand the rain!
(why not, break it down like dat)
'gainst my window (break it down baby)
I can't stand the rain! (uh-huh)
(ya like that? Uh-huh)
I can't stand the rain! (uh, huh)
(ooh, Misdemeanor)
I can't stand the rain!
I can't stand the rain!

Words & Music by Melissa Elliott, Timothy Mosley,
Ann Peebles, Bernard Miller & Don Bryant

© Copyright 1997 JEC Publishing Corporation/
Virginia Beach Music/Mass Confusion Productions/
WB Music Corporation, USA. Warner/Chappell Music Limited (55%)/
Rondor Music (London) Limited (45%).
All Rights Reserved. International Copyright Secured.

Well it's like smack the track up and leave dents in it
The vocalist, bustin' this blunt, instruments spit
The magnificent, rappers run from it
All fly girls, nipples and toes
Numb from it!
MCs in my circumference, is confronted son
Get your growth stunted from this, you don't
want it ('What nigga?')
The Black Thought and M-O-S Def dat done it
Who the ultimate?
Yo my man speak upon it.

[begins with ad-libs]

[Black Thought & Mos Def]
We go wow, ba-da-dow - da-dah-ow
Either stand tall, or sit the fuck down
All the way from the 2-1-5th to Bucktown
Brace yourself, it's about to go down.

[Black Thought]
Yo, Tariq ('Wassup?') how your microphone sound?
('It sound tight')
Well, a'ight, show em what it's about.

[TOGETHER]
We got to blow up the spot, because they
must have forget
We double (trouble) bubble (bubble)
bubble (bubblin' hot).

[Mos Def]
Aiyo! I stop fools and drop jewels but never run it
Rock mics so nice I make your stock
price plummet
All you high noon riders better rally at the summit
It's me and Tariq and your fleet outnumbered
Cross the membrane barking big game and
get hunted

ROOTS
DOUBLE TROUBLE
RELEASED: 1999. INCLUDED ON: THINGS FALL APART (1999)

Eyewitness account, say it happened so sudden
Just slid off to the side, didn't really say nuttin'
Then BLAH!, blew away the 1900th
You better get your rest cos the next day comin'.

[Black Thought]
Oh yes, and MCs they scared to say sum'tin'
Stop frontin', I'm in the cut just onlookin'
Your get your kings, your rooks, rings and pawns
taken.

[Mos Def]
Aiyo! keep your tape rollin'
So you catch every bar of the Black Thought
And the black man from Black Star
Illadelph and Vietnam we conference, accomplish
Even with stakes inclined, I get mine, regardless.

[Black Thought]
Yo, a lot of Smurfette MCs carry purses
And rock, uniforms, that's made for nurses
I burst your verses, your words is worthless
Only touches surface, the fuck's the purpose?

[Mos Def]
What I memorised leave your whole staff
pressurised
Melt down all of your artificial lies
Y'all niggas is faker than Yellow No. 5
Swine like mono and diglyceride
My vocals got texture, you just texturised
I'm nicer than your writtens even when
I'm improvised
Step into my zone get flown like fly by the b-boy
Lazarus who just won't die.

[Black Thought]
Yo, me and Kamal and Leonard Hubbard,
?uestlove and Malik
We go back to dollar hoagies and Tahitian Treat
Or like toast in the oven with government
cheese bubblin'
Me and Dante like Marvin,
The Troublemen travellin'
Give me the mic, we on that again
B-boy business,
Off the top actin' and battlin'
Servin' them cats that forgot
But don't get too close, because you might get shot.

[TOGETHER]
Like bla-ba-dow-da-da-dow-da-dah-ow
Either stand tall or sit the fuck down
All the way from the 2-1-5th to Bucktown
Brace yourself, it's about to go down.

[Mos Def]
Yo, Tariq ('Wassup?') how your microphone sound
('It sound tight')
Well a'ight, show em what it's about.

[TOGETHER]
We 'bout to blow up the spot, because y'all must
have forget
We double (trouble) bubble (bubble) bubble
(bubblin hot)
We go bla-ba-dow-da-da-dow-da-dah-ow
Either stand tall or sit the fuck down
All the way from the 2-1-5th to Bucktown
Went from 'Do You Want More?'
To 'What you want now?'.

[Mos Def]
Yo, Tariq ('Wassup?') how your microphone
sound ('It sound tight')
Well all right, show em what it's about.

[Mos Def]
I shot the sheriff the deputy, and head of
bank treasury
So mounties in the county got a big
bounty stressin' me
But tell 'em to hold off, they too short to
measure me
Mos and Black Thought blast forth with
the weaponry.

[TOGETHER]
Like bla-ba-dow-da-da-dow-da-dah-ow
Either stand tall or sit the fuck down
All the way from the 2-1-5th to Bucktown
Brace yourself, it's about to go down.

[Mos Def]
Yo, Tariq ('Wassup?') how your microphone sound?
('It sound tight')
Well a'ight, show em what it's about.

[TOGETHER]
We got to blow up the spot, because
they must have forget
We double (trouble) bubble (bubble) bubble
(bubblin hot).

[Mos Def]
Yeah, now check your stove top before
you take a listen
And make sure beans don't burn in the kitchen
These gassed-up niggaz just ain't fuel efficient
I play the winter breeze to choke hold your piston
Now you niggas can't make pole position
Class E chassis can't hold the transmission
Crew pit, useless, they got they tools missin'
Watch me, grand prix, champy for wealth driven.

[Black Thought]
Yo, you go one for my hustle (hustle)
Two to rock rhyme (two to rock rhyme)
From the muscle kid I'm one of the illest of all time
I swing from chandeliers and wall climb
And specialize in warfares of all kind
A lot of MCs said I'm a run it down rhyme
But half the time, they run it down one of mine
Thought suffocatin' em with yet another
stunnin' line
You dumb and blind kid, it's enlarged and
underlined.

[TOGETHER]

We 'bout to blow up the spot, because
y'all must have forget
We double (trouble) bubble (bubble)
bubble (bubblin' hot).

[Mos Def]

Say here's a little story that must be told
About two young brothers who got so much soul
They takin' total control, of the body and brain
Flyin' high in the sky, on a lyrical plane
It's just two bad brothers who will never quit
Mos Def and Tariq from the 2-1-5th
They rock beginnin' to end, on a spiritual blend
And everybody who forgot then baby tell 'em again
It's just me and Tariq, with Ahmir on the beat
The Roots crew baby, yo, we got to make it unique
We got the soul-shockinest, body-rockinest
Non-stoppinest
Fortified Live - survive the apocalypse
Rhymes we say, the perfect blend
Because we know how to rock when
the beat come in
Like zen-zen-zen-zen-zen zen-zen-zen-
zen, zen-zen, zen-zen
(repeat)

Here we go, here we, here we, here we go.

Zen zen-zen, zen zen zen zen zen zen
zen zen, zen zen zen-zen
(repeat)

Let the poppers pop, and the breakers break.

Then zen-zen-zen-zen-zen Zen-zen-zen-
zen-zen, zen-zen, zen-zen
(repeat)

Two years ago, a friend of mine . . . (fades)

*Words & Music by Tarik Collins, Ahmir Thompson,
Leonard Hubbard, Jimmy Gray, Dante Smith & James Poyser*
© Copyright 1999 Grand Negaz Music/Jajapo Music, USA.
BMG Music Publishing Limited, Bedford House,
69-79 Fulham High Street, London SW6 3JW (70%)/
Copyright Control (30%).
All Rights Reserved. International Copyright Secured.

ROOTS...

Post-Schoolly D, Philadelphia's finest export has been the Roots, one of the most widely respected, literate and conscientious of hip hop acts. *Things Fall Apart*, the 1999 album which features 'Double Trouble', opens with a short passage transposed from Spike Lee's *Mo' Better Blues* in which the band are berated for being 'grandiose mutherfuckers' who 'don't play shit that [people] like'. That sums up many people's response to the Roots. But the fact that they refuse to conform, offering only staunch musicality and intelligence in the face of the sheepish content of some of their peers, is actually in keeping with hip hop's best traditions.

The group formed in 1987 at Philly's High School For The Creative And Performing Arts, where MC Black Thought hooked up with producer and beat-provider ?uestlove. By 1993, with the addition of a bass player, Leonard 'Hub' Hubbard and second MC Malik B, they cut their independent debut, *Organix*. Taking their cue from Gang Starr's forays into rap-jazz, they experimented with live instruments instead of samples, a theory taken to the max on 1995's breakthrough album *Do You Want More?!!!??!*, which was entirely sample-free, and *Illadelph Halflife* a year later. By this time they'd established themselves as one of the most engaging and energetic live acts of the post-Public Enemy era, and were widely regarded as a 'progressive' force in hip hop.

But it all came together on *Things Fall Apart*. Its title was taken from Chinua Achebe's book on colonialism, and it featured a fine collaboration with Erykah Badu on 'You Got Me', as well as guest spots for rapper Common and R&B star D'Angelo. Then there was 'Double Trouble', a frentically-paced old-school styled tag team tie-up between Black Thought and underground superstar Mos Def. It was the last song to be recorded for an album that was boiled down from nearly 150 demo tracks – many created as a result of 'jam sessions', a real rarity in hip hop. As the sleevenotes acknowledge, Def's Black Star partner Talib Kweli had originally performed some vocals, before Black Thought decided he wanted a 'Run-D.M.C. '85 tug of war style' finished article. While the song is a self-conscious throwback to the freestyling traditions of old school MCs, the musical backing was designed to recreate the percussion punch of an old Marley Marl record. And, like so many things in the Roots' canon, it works beautifully.

Hi!
My name is... (What?)
My name is... (Who?)
My name is... [SCRATCHING] Slim Shady!
Hi!
My name is... (Huh?)
My name is... (What?)
My name is... [SCRATCHING] Slim Shady!

Ahem... excuse me!
Can I have the attention of the class for one second?
Hi, kids! Do you like violence? (Yeah, yeah, yeah!)
Wanna see me stick nine inch nails through each
one of my eyelids? (A-ha!)
Wanna copy me and do exactly like I did?
(Yeah, yeah!)
Try 'cid and get fucked up worse that my life is?
(Huh?)
My brain's dead weight, I'm tryin' to
get my head straight

Hi!
My name is... (What?)
My name is... (Who?)
My name is... [SCRATCHING] Slim Shady!
Hi!
My name is... (Huh?)
My name is... (What?)
My name is... [SCRATCHING] Slim Shady!

My English teacher wanted to flunk me in
junior high
Thanks a lot, next semester I'll be 35
I smacked him in his face with an eraser
Chased him with a stapler and stapled his nuts
to a stack of papers (Ow!)
Walked in the strip club, had my jacket zipped up
Flashed the bartender, then stuck my dick in the
tip cup

EMINEM

MY NAME IS

RELEASED: 1999. INCLUDED ON: THE SLIM SHADY LP (1999)

but I can't figure out which Spice Girl
I want to impregnate (Umm...)
And Dr Dre said, 'Slim Shady you a basehead!'
Uh-uhh!
'So why's your face red? Man you wasted!'
Well since age twelve, I've felt like I'm someone else
Cos I hung my original self from the top
bunk with a belt
Got pissed off and ripped Pamela Lee's tits off
And smacked her so hard I knocked her clothes
backwards like Kris Kross
I smoke a fat pound of grass and fall on my ass
Faster than a fat bitch who sat down too fast
Come here, slut!
(Shady, wait a minute, that's my girl, dog!)
I don't give a fuck, God sent me to piss the
world off!

Extraterrestrial, runnin' over pedestrians
in a spaceship
While they screamin' at me: "Let's just be friends!"
99 per cent of my life I was lied to
I just found out my mom does more dope
than I do (Damn!)
I told her I'd grow up to be a famous rapper
Make a record about doin' drugs and name it
after her (Oh, thank you!)
You know you blew up when the women rush
your stands
And try to touch your hands like some screamin'
Usher fans (SCREAMING)
This guy at White Castle asked for my autograph
(Dude, can I get your autograph?)
So I signed it: 'Dear Dave, thanks for the
support, asshole!'.

Hi!
My name is... (What?)
My name is... (Who?)
My name is... [SCRATCHING] Slim Shady!

EMINEM...

Several people have become very rich by using rap music to stir controversy, but Eminem upped the ante every time he opened his filthy, smart-ass mouth. Every responsible parent's nightmare, he is a physical personification of the screw-you-ethos of post-slacker don't-wannabes. The first authentic white rap star, Marshall Mathers grew up as a card-carrying member of America's white trailer trash underclass. He distracted himself by improvising freestyle raps, immediately discovering he had a talent for kickin' rhymes. He supported himself by flipping burgers and cleaning toilets while releasing a couple of independent records that went nowhere. He first showed up on the media's radar with his *Slim Shady EP* of 1997. Signature song 'Just Don't Give A Fuck' announced an agenda rooted in morbid misanthropy and gallows humour, a worldview that west coast gangsta linchpin Dr Dre had some knowledge of. As a result of Dre's patronage Eminem secured a contract with Interscope Records.

'My Name Is' was the lead single from his debut album proper, *The Slim Shady LP*. Completed in tandem with Dre (who produced three tracks), its musical core was provided by 'an interpolation' of Labi Siffre's 'I Got The', over which Eminem rapid-fired his dislocated, comic-absurd meditations – incorporating references to Pamela Anderson's bosom, former kiddie rappers Kriss Kross's inverted wardrobe, and impregnating Spice Girls. However, all that's topped by a shout-out to his loving ma – 'I just found out my mom does more dope than I do' – that resulted in mater issuing a writ against her errant firstborn for defamation. The song is closed out by Eminem's dreams of slitting his father's throat.

Eminem was the Sex Pistols reincarnated as a hip hop act (the fact that he combined Sid's nihilistic, dopey nonchalance with Lydon's burning intelligence and resentment helped). He soon became a regular on current affairs programmes surpassing even Marilyn Manson as the focus of international moral indignation.

Eminem, unlike 2 Live Crew and their ilk, was more than just a parent-baiting cartoon, or Beavis and Butthead made flesh. Beneath the bad-ass badinage lay one of the best lyricists to emerge in the last 20 years, a skilled MC who'd paid dues on the freestylin' circuit (so much so that he still rages, even after all these years and album sales, about being 'cheated' of victory in the 1997 Rap Olympics). We have not heard the last, or possibly the best, of him yet.

EMINEM

Hi!
My name is... (Huh?)
My name is... (What?)
My name is... [SCRATCHING] Slim Shady!

Stop the tape! This kid needs to be
locked away! (Get him!)
Dr Dre, don't just stand there, operate!
I'm not ready to leave, it's too scary to die
(Fuck that!)
I'll have to be carried inside the cemetery
and buried alive (Huh yeah!)
Am I comin' or goin'? I can barely decide
I just drank a fifth of vodka – dare me to drive?
(Go ahead)
All my life I was very deprived,
I ain't had a woman in years
My palms are too hairy to hide (Whoops!)
Clothes ripped like the Incredible Hulk (SUCKS
UP SPITTLE AND SPITS)
I spit when I talk, I'll fuck anything that walks
(Come 'ere!)
When I was little I used to get so hungry
I would throw fits –
How you gonna breastfeed me, Mom?
You ain't got no tits! (Wah! Wah!)
I lay awake and strap myself in the bed
Put a bulletproof vest on and shoot myself
in the head (BANG)
I'm steamin' mad (Argh!)
And by the way when you see my dad? (Yeah?)
Tell him that I slit his throat, in this dream I had.

Hi!
My name is... (What?)
My name is... (Who?)
My name is... [SCRATCHING] Slim Shady!
Hi!
My name is... (Huh?)
My name is... (What?)
My name is... [SCRATCHING] Slim Shady!

(Repeat)

Words by Marshall Mathers & Andre Young
Music by Labi Siffre

[Rainfall]

[Dido]
My tea's gone cold I'm wondering why
I got out of bed at all
The morning rain clouds up my window
And I can't see at all
And even if I could it'll all be grey
But your picture on my wall
It reminds me, that it's not so bad, it's not so bad
(x2).

[Eminem as 'Stan']
Dear Slim, I wrote you but you still ain't callin'
I left my cell, my pager, and my home
phone at the bottom
I sent two letters back in autumn,
you must not-a got 'em
There probably was a problem at the
post office or somethin'

[Eminem as 'Stan']
Dear Slim, you still ain't called or wrote
I hope you have a chance
I ain't mad –
I just think it's fucked up you don't answer fans
If you didn't wanna talk to me outside your
concert you didn't have to,
but you coulda signed an autograph for Matthew
That's my little brother man, he's only six years old
We waited in the blistering cold for you
Four hours and you just said, 'No.'
That's pretty shitty man – you're like his fuckin' idol
He wants to be just like you man, he likes you
more than I do
I ain't that mad though, I just don't like being lied to
Remember when we met in Denver –
You said if I'd write you, you would write back
See I'm just like you in a way
I never knew my father neither

EMINEM

STAN

RELEASED: 2000. INCLUDED ON: THE MARSHALL MATHERS LP (2000)

EMINEM

Sometimes I scribble addresses too sloppy
when I jot 'em
But anyways, fuck it, what's been up, man,
how's your daughter?
My girlfriend's pregnant too, I'm bout to be a father
If I have a daughter, guess what I'ma call her?
I'ma name her Bonnie
I read about your Uncle Ronnie too
I'm sorry
I had a friend kill himself over some
bitch who didn't want him
I know you probably hear this every day
But I'm your biggest fan
I even got the underground shit that
you did with Skam
I got a room full of your posters and
your pictures man
I like the shit you did with Rawkus too,
that shit was phat
Anyways, I hope you get this man
Hit me back, just to chat, truly yours,
your biggest fan
This is Stan.

[Dido chorus]

He used to always cheat on my mom and beat her
I can relate to what you're saying in your songs
So when I have a shitty day
I drift away and put 'em on
Cos I don't really got shit else so that shit
helps when I'm depressed
I even got a tattoo of your name across the chest
Sometimes I even cut myself to see how much it bleeds
It's like adrenaline, the pain is such a sudden rush for me
See everything you say is real, and I respect
you cos you tell it
My girlfriend's jealous cos I talk about you 24/7
But she don't know you like I know you Slim,
no-one does
She don't know what it was like for people
like us growing up
You gotta call me man,
I'll be the biggest fan you'll ever lose
Sincerely yours, Stan –
P.S. We should be together too.

[Dido chorus]

[Eminem as 'Stan']

Dear Mister-I'm-Too-Good-To-Call-Or-
Write-My-Fans
This'll be the last package I ever send your ass
It's been six months and still no word –
I don't deserve it?
I know you got my last two letters
I wrote the addresses on 'em perfect
So this is my cassette I'm sending you,
I hope you hear it
I'm in the car right now, I'm doing 90 on the freeway
Hey Slim, I drank a fifth of vodka,
you dare me to drive?
You know the song by Phil Collins,
'In the Area Tonight?'
About that guy who coulda saved that
other guy from drowning but didn't?
Then Phil saw it all, then at a show he found him?
That's kinda how this is, you coulda
rescued me from drowning
Now it's too late – I'm on a 1,000 downers now,
I'm drowsy
And all I wanted was a lousy letter or a call
I hope you know I ripped all of your
pictures off the wall
I love you Slim, we coulda been together
Think about it
You ruined it now, I hope you can't sleep
and you dream about it
And when you dream I hope you can't sleep
and you scream about it
I hope your conscience eats at you and
you can't breathe without me
See Slim...
[Screaming]
Shut up bitch! I'm tryin' to talk!
Hey Slim, that's my girlfriend screamin' in the trunk
But I didn't slit her throat, I just tied her up
See I ain't like you cos if she suffocates
she'll suffer more
And then she'll die too
Well, gotta go, I'm almost at the bridge now
Oh shit, I forgot, how am I supposed to
send this shit out?

[Squeal of tyres and crash]
[Dido chorus]

[Eminem]
Dear Stan, I meant to write you sooner
but I just been busy
You said your girlfriend's pregnant now,
how far along is she?
Look, I'm really flattered you would
call your daughter that
And here's an autograph for your brother
I wrote it on the Starter cap
I'm sorry I didn't see you at the show,
I musta missed you
Don't think I did that shit intentionally
just to diss you
But what's this shit you said about you
like to cut your wrists too?
I say that shit just clownin', dog, c'mon –
how fucked up is you?
You got some issues, Stan,
I think you need some counselling
To help your ass from bouncing off the
walls when you get down some
And what's this shit about us meant to be together?
That type of shit'll make me not want us to
meet each other
I really think you and your girlfriend need each other
Or maybe you just need to treat her better
I hope you get to read this letter
I just hope it reaches you in time before you
hurt yourself
I think that you'll be doin' just fine if you relax a little
I'm glad I inspire you, but Stan, why are you so mad?
Try to understand, that I do want you as a fan
I just don't want you to do some crazy shit
I seen this one shit on the news a couple weeks
ago that made me sick
Some dude was drunk and drove his car over a bridge
And had his girlfriend in the trunk
And she was pregnant with his kid
And in the car they found a tape
But they didn't say who it was to.

Come to think about, his name was...
It was you.
Damn!

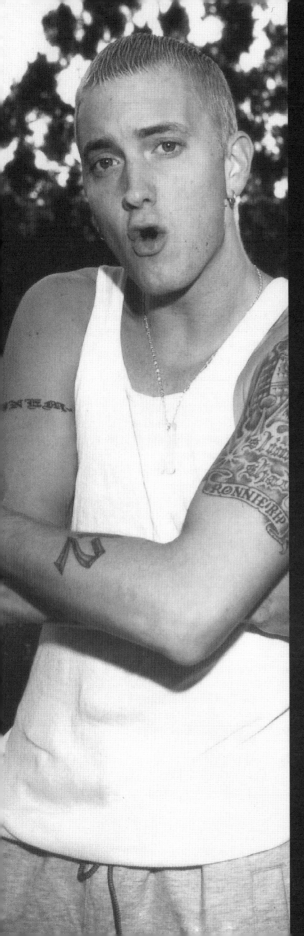

STAN...

'Stan', the first great commercial single of the new millennium, suggested that maybe Public Enemy had got it wrong. Maybe we should believe the hype.

A haunting tirade narrated by a disgruntled fan who wants to live his life through his foul-mouthed hero, 'Stan' is part-confessional, part-Stephen King horror homage, part-Jacobean tragedy. Only a couple of years before its release Eminem was admitting in interviews that: 'I hope I do influence people. I want somebody to be able to look up to me and say I want to rap like you, I want to be like you, I want to do this like you.' Now he was contextualising, if not wholly backing away from, his responsibilities.

The song was co-produced by the 45 King, one of hip hop's legendary producers. The finished track liberally employs the hook to then unknown artist Dido's 'Thank You', in turn launching her career as most-played-artist on the 2001 dinner party circuit. She was suitably impressed when she got to meet the rapper: 'What shocked me about him is just how seriously he takes it and how devoted he is. He is mortified if he fucks up a line.'

Even former detractors found it hard to criticise the strength of a lyric which topped the charts in both Britain and America. Structured episodically around letters to the artist, it employed a number of clever narrative devices, not least the advice in Eminem's eventual reply that 'Stan' find some counselling and get in touch with his feelings – how very Oprah of the most despised artist working in popular music. Stan's distracted logic as he bemoans his handwriting skills as a possible excuse for the non-appearance of Eminem's reply reveals the author's eye for detail, especially when essaying the 'white trash' characters that populated his own youth, while the reference to Phil Collins' profundity is pulled off with such skill you hardly notice it first time round.

'Stan', its cinematic storyline augmented by a claustrophobic, rainswept video, boasts the same tall-tale aesthetic of namesake Stan Ridgeway's 'Camouflage' without ever descending into Kenny Rogers-like bathos. 'Stan' was the song that finally established Eminem, who'd milked the wanton, morally vacuous puppet rap star role for all its worth, as a thinking, sentient artist.

May I have your attention please?
May I have your attention please?
Will the real Slim Shady please stand up?
I repeat, will the real Slim Shady please stand up?
We're gonna have a problem here.

Y'all act like you never seen a white person before
Jaws all on the floor like Pam
Like Tommy just burst in the door
And started whoopin' her ass worse than
before they first were divorced
Throwin' her over furniture (Ah!)

It's the return of the...
'Ah, wait, no way, you're kidding,
he didn't just say what I think he did, did he?'
And Dr Dre said... nothing you idiots!
Dr Dre's dead, he's locked in my basement! (Ha-ha!)
Feminist women love Eminem
'Slim Shady, I'm sick of him'
Look at him, walkin' around grabbin' his
you-know-what
Flippin' the you-know-who,"
'Yeah, but he's so cute though!'
Yeah, I probably got a couple of screws
up in my head loose
But no worse than what's goin' on in
your parents' bedrooms
Sometimes, I wanna get on TV and just let loose
But can't but it's cool for Tom Green to
hump a dead moose
'My bum is on your lips, my bum is on your lips'
And if I'm lucky, you might just give it a little kiss
And that's the message that we deliver to little kids
And expect them not to know what a
woman's clitoris is
Of course they gonna know what intercourse is
By the time they hit fourth grade
They got the Discovery Channel don't they?
We ain't nothing but mammals..
Well, some of us cannibals who cut other
people open like cantaloupes
But if we can hump dead animals and antelopes
Then there's no reason that a man and
another man can't elope
But if you feel like I feel, I got the antidote
Women wave your pantyhose,
sing the chorus and it goes –

I'm Slim Shady, yes I'm the real Shady
All you other Slim Shadys are just imitating
So won't the real Slim Shady please stand up,
please stand up, please stand up? (x2)

Will Smith don't gotta cuss in his raps to sell records
Well I do, so fuck him and fuck you too!
You think I give a damn about a Grammy?
Half of you critics can't even stomach me,
let alone stand me
'But Slim, what if you win, wouldn't it be weird?'
Why? So you guys could just lie to get me here?
So you can sit me here next to Britney Spears?
Shit, Christina Aguilera better switch me chairs
So I can sit next to Carson Daly and Fred Durst
And hear 'em argue over who she gave head to first
You little bitch, put me on blast on MTV
'Yeah, he's cute, but I think he's married
to Kim, hee-hee!'
I should download her audio on MP3
And show the whole world how you gave
Eminem VD.

I just get on the mic and spit it and whether
you like to admit it
I just shit it better than ninety percent of
you rappers out can
Then you wonder how can kids eat up these
albums like valiums
It's funny: cos at the rate I'm goin' when I'm thirty
I'll be the only person in the nursing home flirtin'
Pinchin' nurses asses when I'm jackin'
off with Jergens
And I'm jerkin' but this whole bag of
Viagra isn't working
And every single person is a Slim Shady lurkin'
He could be workin' at Burger King, spittin'
on your onion rings
Or in the parkin' lot, circling
Screaming 'I don't give a fuck!'
With his windows down and his system up
So, will the real Shady please stand up?
And put one of those fingers on each hand up?

EMINEM
THE REAL SLIM SHADY
RELEASED: 2000. INCLUDED ON: THE MARSHALL MATHERS LP (2000)

EMINEM

I'm sick of you little girl and boy groups,
all you do is annoy me
So I have been sent here to destroy you
And there's a million of us just like me
who cuss like me
Who just don't give a fuck like me
Who dress like me
Walk, talk and act like me
And just might be the next best thing
But not quite me!

I'm Slim Shady, yes I'm the real Shady
All you other Slim Shadys are just imitating
So won't the real Slim Shady please stand up,
please stand up, please stand up? (x2)

I'm like a head trip to listen to
Cos I'm only givin' you things you joke
about with your friends
Inside your living room
The only difference is I got the balls to
say it in front of y'all
And I don't gotta be false or sugarcoated at all

And be proud to be outta your mind and
outta control
And one more time
Loud as you can, how does it go?

I'm Slim Shady, yes I'm the real Shady
All you other Slim Shadys are just imitating
So won't the real Slim Shady please stand up,
please stand up, please stand up? (x4)

Ha ha
Guess there's a Slim Shady in all of us
Fuck it, let's all stand up.

Words & Music by Marshall Mathers, Andre Young,
Mike Elizondo & Thomas Coster

© Copyright 2000 Eight Mile Style/Ensign Music
Corporation/Famous Music Corporation (50%)/Ain't Nothin'
*Goin' On But F****n' Music/Five Card Music/*
Elvis Mambo Music/Strawberry Blonde Music, USA.
Windswept Music (London) Limited, Hope House, 40 St. Peter's
Road, London W6 9BD (20%)/Bug Music Limited, 31 Milson Road,
London W14 0LJ (20%)/Warner/Chappell Music Limited,
Griffin House, 161 Hammersmith Road, London W6 8BS (10%).
All Rights Reserved. International Copyright Secured.

THE REAL SLIM SHADY...

With its distinctive Haunted House keyboard intro and mental institution video setting, 'The Real Slim Shady' is one of Eminem's keynote addresses, offering a card sharp's clues as to the real identity of its author.

Playing with Eminem's public persona, 'The Real Slim Shady' dovetails with 'Marshall Mathers' to provide an understanding of the kid who grow'd up beat'up in Detroit and discovered a natural, Satan-given talent for rapping – a white guy discovering and devouring black culture. Throughout his career Eminem's had to defend himself against vapid accusations that he's the new Vanilla Ice (the new Beastie Boys, perhaps). Even his mentor Dr Dre had to admit to *Rolling Stone* that it all felt a bit weird. 'It's like seeing a black guy doing some country & western, know what I mean?'

So who is the Real Slim Shady? It's a guise Eminem first adopted on the *Slim Shady* EP in 1998. Shady serves as a kind of hip hop homunculus, a defence mechanism that deflects criticism while the puppetmaster laughs at the wanton destruction and media hyperventilation that ensues. As Eminem elucidates, 'every single person is a Slim Shady lurkin'/He could be workin' at Burger King, spittin' on your onion rings'.

Eminem came up with 'The Real Slim Shady' at the request of Interscope, who were looking for a new single. He and Dr Dre spent several fruitless hours exhausting themselves trying to fit a beat to the lyric. 'I was tellin' the bass player and keyboard player to keep playing till I liked it. So they kept fuckin' around... till Tommy [Coster Jr, Dre's keyboard player] played the first few notes of 'The Real Slim Shady' and I jumped up and said, "What was that?"'. The lyrics were partially inspired by Christine Aguilera's comments about Eminem on MTV (specifically the fact that he was married, a status he didn't want revealed) and Will Smith's comments about gangsta rap and 'all that cussing'. It's one of several tracks on the album to lash out at manufactured boy bands and girl groups, the artifice of the Grammy Awards, and music critics. Eminem clearly has little use for any of these, though the truth is he's as widely admired as he is reviled.